Only Believe

CAROL ANDERSON

Ark House Press
arkhousepress.com

Cataloguing in Publication Data:
Title: Only Believe
ISBN: 978-1-7644430-1-2 (pbk)
Subjects: REL012170 RELIGION / Christian Living / Personal Memoirs; REL012120 RELIGION / Christian Living / Spiritual Growth; REL012040 RELIGION / Christian Living / Inspirational.

Design by initiateagency.com

PERSONAL TESTIMONIES

You cannot read this book without being immersed in the weight of its pure and beautiful anointing. Every word and page carries the fragrance and presence of precious Holy Spirit, flowing like holy oil directly from heaven. This is not just another work of Christian fiction—it is a prophetic encounter that revives the soul and awakens a deeper hunger for intimate fellowship with God.

Carol writes each sentence out of her own profoundly personal and intimate walk with the Lord, birthing something truly beautiful and sacred.

Sarah

I have just finished reading your beautiful book. Loved it! My heart is still fluttering from reading it.

This divinely inspired story invites you into the deeply vulnerable and sacred space of Katie's secret place with her LORD.

As the delicately choreographed words unfold like a beautiful dance of intimacy, you will be drawn along with Katie on a journey of deep love, extravagant worship, and ultimately facing the deepest question, and fear of many of our hearts… "Am I enough?"

You will laugh, cry and be inspired to go deeper yet again in the LORD as you become immersed in Katie's quest to know the Truth, and ultimately experience the freedom to be who she knows He has made her to be.

Rachel

Wow such a blessing from the LORD, the book is beautiful! Carol writes amazing and relatable characters; her writing comes from a very personal and intimate place. She is walking in her talent and to God be all the glory.

Breie

I had the privilege of watching this book unfold week by week as the normality of life became supernaturally alive by the presence of HIM (the lover of our soul). This is far more than a fictitious book it is a living experience teaching you how to walk day by day with the great I AM.

Carol lives her life daily entwined in the LORD. He is her everything. She carries a strong prophetic and teaching mantle that will transform your soul and spirit as you read this book bringing healing direction and new faith.

ONLY BELIEVE challenges you to invite the God of love into your everyday life and see HIM beautifully transform every situation.

ENJOY THE JOURNEY

Rea

I loved your book; it is very inspiring and a love letter to the LORD and back to us. Well done, Carol.

Marilyn

Beautifully written, with a real knowledge of God's heart, a feeling of passion, warmth and love throughout. Well done Carol on another great book.

Janette

DEDICATION

This book is dedicated entirely with love and thanks to The One True and Living God and The Son whom He sent and Lovely Holy Spirit.

It is You who gave me a gift to read and write - and a passion for Your Word – you taught me…Thank You.

I have not always journeyed well but always – You picked me up and have been all things for me – with your constant love.

Only Believe – The title is all I received at first for this book and each week I knew He would reveal what I was to write. Not always comfortable with it…

I was kept wondering with the way He would lead and the journey He had, not only for the readers – but for me as a writer.

My passion is always for deeper intimacy, as someone mentioned who read *Only Believe*, the manuscript, it's like the robe has been removed.

Love is obedience.

ACKNOWLEDGEMENTS

To my beautiful Spiritual son and daughter Dave and Breie. I love you both so much and your precious daughters, Teeghan and Baby Peace. I love this gift of family love Mumma Carol. You all have a special place in my heart.

To Matthew, who without his help the manuscript would never have made it to the publisher, he helped me every step of the way. God bless your kindness and all the time you gave to me… you are truly a treasure.

To my friends who helped with the editing; beautiful Breie with her inspirational writing styles and precious Rachel, for your love and encouragement.

My love and thanks to Emily and Jess for their friendship that grows deeper every year.

My friend Rea, who is playful and fun – love being with you in the Glory, going places beyond our imaginations.

For James and Nicole at Ark House Publishing, you brought this gift to life with the gifts on your lives. Nicole, I love what you did with the cover on both of my books. James, thank you from the first phone call you have been so helpful to simplify the process of giving my books wings. Thank you.

Many and sincere thanks to my precious LORD Jesus, the Good Shepherd for the financial blessing and those that He moved upon to sow. Thank you all.

All scripture has been placed in ***italics*** and ***centred,***
and all songs have been **centred.**

CONTENTS

CHAPTER 1

The Dream

Katie opened her eyes as she felt the fabric of the sheets with her fingertips, just the touch alone convincing her she was truly present in the moment. The powerful moment between sleep and awake. She closed her eyes and heard the same Voice as she had so clearly in her dream, she never saw a face or a person, just the Voice that resonated through her. A Voice of such authority, a Voice that caused her to tremble. A Voice that she had longed to hear all her life and yet, it terrified her.

It was God, Himself, the one her heart adored, but not in the sweetness, the gentleness but the full power of who He is, or at least what He knew she could receive at that time. And over and over she heard His Voice, His Words as He questioned her, it's like her heart had been opened and exposed; like a sword was still inside her.

In the dream she did not answer, nor could she now; His question was so deep and large, it was so high and lofty. He was provoking her to search inside and see her faith and trust and love for Him. The magnitude of the question was on so many levels mind blowing and over whelming and yet it should have been simple. The weightiness of it, caused her to wish she could fly away and find rest. It was so deep and as she breathed, knowing He was in the room, she was breathing the very breath of Him.

She slowly dropped down out of the bed and knelt before the invisible God whose presence was glorious and lower she knelt and had her eyes been open to see at that moment, her face was touching His feet, she wept all over them.

THE FEAR OF THE LORD IS THE BEGINNING OF WISDOM.

Hours had passed, in silence as Katie lay right beside her bed, face down waiting, wondering what to do. She slowly reached behind her to the bedside table and grasped the books that she knew would be there. The Bible, The Word of God, she drew one near and before thoughts were on her tongue, He answered them. Katie was stunned as she opened the book to the very page, the very verse that He had just impressed upon her heart. 'How did You do that?'

She read the scripture aloud in awe and wonder:

> *Your eyes saw my unformed substance, and in Your book all the days of my life were written, before they ever took shape, when as yet, there was none of them.*

She reached again behind her for another Bible and opened immediately to the same verse and read it aloud:

> *Your eyes saw my unformed body, all the days ordained for me were written in Your book before one of them came to be.*

She then pulled the old faithful Bible she had loved as a young believer in the LORD to the carpet and opened again at the very page and verse, totally blown away by what He was doing:

> *You saw me before I was born and scheduled each day of my life before I began to breathe. Every day was recorded in Your book!*

As she listened to the prompt in her heart, knowing He was not just leading her but teaching her, she turned the pages and found what she was looking for. *'I know the plans I have for you, declares the LORD.'* Katie felt such a stir to arise and go to her keyboard. She pressed the chords and experienced the wonder of His presence so powerfully that it brought her to tears. As she opened her mouth her heart was so consumed with love for Him.

What do you say to one you don't see? As she thought about it, she gushed, "The same thing you say to the one you do see. I love You… Jesus, I love You." All she wanted was this moment, this meeting with Him on such a sweet level, singing out: "I love You; I love You; I love You."

And somewhere in the distance she heard a phone ringing taking her attention away, she tried to ignore it, but it was quickly followed by voices and a loud knock at her front door. "Oh God stay with me," she poured out of the depths of her being, wiping the tears from her face. It was then she remembered she was still in her night dress, so she called, "I won't be a moment," and quickly went back to her bedroom to change.

Such special friends and yet she was lost in her own thoughts and not willing to share what had been taking place. She went through the motions of making coffee and breaking open a packet of biscuits and listened as they all shared their week and invited her out to the Light House. In her spirit she heard the gentle word, "Go."

In her reasoning it made no sense at all as all she wanted was to be alone with Him, but peace came upon her heart and mind, so she smiled as she replied, "I'd love too."

THE LIGHT HOUSE

They all left in one car and sang all the way to the Light House, old and new songs that they all loved. Four unique individuals, drawn together by the LORD. The greatest thing they all had in common was their love for Him. All of them from different backgrounds and even different countries. Their personal testimonies so vastly different, their careers and education. Three of them had been married. Two of them had children. But all four of them were now, living alone. Divorce and death had changed the landscape of their happily ever after. The grief and loneliness had affected all of them, they were not the same women they once were, but that was the past.

> "This is my desire to honour You, LORD with all my heart I worship You, all I have within me I give You praise, all that I adore is in You."

With their windows down they sang out the songs not only for the LORD but with the intent that passing cars would hear the words and be touched by the Joy of the LORD.

> "LORD, I give You my heart I give You my soul, I
> live for You alone, with every breath that I take, every
> moment I'm awake, LORD have Your way in me."

What felt like no time at all they had arrived at the carpark of the Light House and made their way along the path. There was such a beautiful warmth to the day even with the gentle breeze. Everything looked so green and alive all the trees, the plants all different shades of green, even some native flowers, it was breath taking.

Nothing compared with the incredible view as they reached the top of the stairs and looked out to the horizon and ocean. The sound of the ocean and the birds, even the air around them seemed to carry a frequency all its own. It was like stepping into a different realm, a place where everything was possible, and you could dream larger and hope for greater. Katie watched as her friends all walked along paths alone, up high on the cliff, thinking their own thoughts, praying, or merely remaining caught up in the beauty. Something they all enjoyed about each other was they never needed to be in each other's company continually to be content. It was like an unspoken word that they all could go out together and yet have space.

Katie chose to sit on the rocks near the cliff face overlooking the island, the ocean, and the enormous blue sky. Massive waves were crashing, and dolphins were riding them and jumping completely out of the waves, the timing of arriving to see that, made her smile. She noticed couples and dogs walking near her. She heard them as they passed, but her mind was on Him. The way His Voice had made her tremble, and the question He had asked.

This morning was so normal, so natural, sleeping, waking even right here in this place with her friends. But it wasn't normal or natural, He changed everything with His Holy Spirit, and it became super - natural. He had gently commanded her to "Go." She played with the rocks, with her fingers as she meditated on His word, fidgeting used to always ease her when she was anxious or concerned about something but not this time. Her mind darting from one thought to another. She slowly stood to her feet, with a small handful of rocks ready to cast them as she cast her cares, her fears. Tears gently began to fall.

So intent on what she was doing she never noticed a young girl come and sit down beside her. Then suddenly, she felt someone touch her hand and got a surprise to see a pretty little girl about five smiling up at her. Katie turned her head quickly to see where her parents were and assumed it was the couple closest to them. She smiled at them and gave them a gentle nod as if to say, 'she's okay with me.'

The little girl held her hand and reached out to take the last small stone from her other hand. Katie felt the stone was smooth, oval, and looked at it, it was white, with flecks of grey and black, not like the others at her feet. Without hesitation Katie gave it to her, and the little girl smiled even broader. The little girl stood up and faced the ocean, both, hand in hand. Then just as quietly she let go of her hand and the little girl suddenly turned and walked away without a word spoken. Katie watched her as she climbed up the path but was even more puzzled as she walked not toward the couple closest to her but toward the Light House. Her curiosity was peaked and her sense of care for a little girl wandering alone, so she began to follow her. It was then as she was nearing the Light House that her friends were making their way toward her.

"Hey, did you see a little girl I was just sitting with?" Katie asked as they all caught up.

"You weren't sitting with a little girl," one of the ladies replied.

"Yeah, I was just sitting with a little girl, maybe you couldn't see," Katie stated.

"Katie, we have all been up at the Light house we could see you for the last little while, no one was with you."

"Did you see me throwing rocks?"

"Yes, you were alone." They all emphasized.

Katie ran toward the Light House and all around it. She looked in all directions, though it was the perfect vantage point to see, they were right.

There was no little girl. On the walk back along the path to the carpark, Shelley caught up with Katie and fell into step with her. It was an awkward silence until Shelley asked, "Do you want to talk?"

Katie shook her head without looking at her and quietly said, "No, I need to process with the LORD."

Shelley remained silent and waited. A bird was singing somewhere in the bushland, and then another bird chirped, a noisy minor and a butcher bird joined in. On their own, their voices were not so pretty, but together it was beautiful. Then the squawking of a rainbow lorikeet accompanied them.

"Do you suppose this is what the LORD hears as we all lift our voices and sing together?" Shelley asked.

"I thought it was real; I thought she was real," Katie stammered, revealing the thoughts of her heart.

"She is real, angels are real," Shelley spoke with such joy in her voice.

"She was a little girl."

"No, she was a Messenger, and we all know you saw something, judging by your behaviour now."

"So, what was her great message?" Katie spoke out a little too harshly.

"You already know!"

Katie felt like the blood was draining from her face.

"But she never spoke to me." Katie's words came out in a whisper.

"Maybe she didn't need too. What were you doing?"

"Sounds silly now," Katie looked at her hands. "I was speaking out my cares as I cast rocks to the ocean below, but she wanted the last one."

"Did she cast it for you?" Shelley asked enjoying the mystery.

Katie shook her head, "she took it with her."

"Well then, perhaps it wasn't a care or a worry but simply the way you were looking at it… just a thought."

Katie felt goosebumps go all over her body, like even her hair was standing on end.

CHAPTER 2

Confessions of the Heart

Weeks had passed since that day since the dream. Katie walked so gently trying not to leave an imprint as her heart and mind were still drawn back to the moment He had entered.

The sun was pouring through the slightly parted curtains in her bedroom, her quiet sanctuary where she sat upon her bed with the Bible open, just looking at it with such awe.

"I'm afraid of You. Yet I'm so in love, like it makes no sense. I feel like I don't want to take a step, in case I miss You, or get it wrong, and I will, as only You are perfect. I want to come so close and experience so much, and yet I feel like I have been keeping You at a distance. I love You; do You know that? And I really fear You. It's what I've always wanted, to really fear You, teach me how to walk with You now."

Katie turned her music on but immediately knew it wasn't the right sound. She walked out to the lounge room and picked up her guitar and her tuner and made her way back to her room. "Is this what You want?"

"All my thoughts are about You. I open the pages of Your Word and want to come closer; I want to wrap them around me or be like the prophet who ate them, sweet to the taste, but I feel edgy and brittle. Like my life is still going but I'm stuck, and I don't really understand it. It's because of the dream, it's because of what You asked me, isn't it?"

LOVE IS OBEDIENCE

Katie strummed her guitar and sang in the spirit, pouring out her heart and the heart she yearned to have, deeper for Him.

> "I know You hear me, I know You're listening, I know You're watching me, Your eyes upon me, I pray my eyes be upon You. Oh, that I might see You, see Your beautiful face, Your eyes, Your mouth, to look at Your hands."

Just the thought of the words she sang to Him, made her heart even more tender. She continued to strum softly.

> "You say, love is obedience, You say, love is obedience, You say, oh precious Lord, You said it, Love is obedience. We look at the cross, we look at Your hands, we see You lifted high, love is obedience… And in our hearts with closed eyes, imaginations flowing, we picture You."

> "Father, I love You, I love You, I sing to You."

Katie closed her eyes and sang.

> "This is the love song I came to find whilst laying at His feet. It was His every Word sang out since the beginning of time. Every Word is Him and draws me deeper into the melody of Him.

He sang out the thoughts of His heart; an orchestra played each breath of Him. He spoke life into every living thing. It all serenades Him. He created the beauty and wonder of everything, and it all reflects Him.

He sang a Love song of faithfulness and everlasting love, and He chose those who drew close to Him to write His song. He revealed Himself and opened Himself up, that others may know Him- love Him.

I listened and the notes became softer clawing at my heart, only the sound of strings remained to record His tears, as His people stepped away from Him, all through the ages, all through the years.

And still He sang on, into an endless night- clinging to the hope they would find Him again and want Him, more than what they had in this world.

He created a new song to welcome them in, and the pages grew as the Love of Him was written across each verse each chapter. He blessed them and showered them in gifts and Words of love, but they could not see His face, they could not hear His heart ache ... because they had not allowed Him in their hearts.

He watched them in their sin, and heard them when they cried, and He saw their sorrow and pain, and He saw their sickness, and His heart broke for them.

And the Word became flesh for them and His body the love song. And a new sound was played out as the whip lashed across His back and His blood sprinkled to the ground.

Healed by His stripes, it sang, healed by His stripes, and thirty-nine times penetrated the darkness, of the lives of His people, and they were healed of every sickness and disease. And some believed in Him and looked upon His face.

All these years have passed, and I lay me down at His feet, and yet I have never seen the beauty of His face.
I hide away where they pierced Him, and I have perfect peace up against His heart, and His blood still pours out over me.

Forgiven and washed clean, and into a hurting world I hear His Love song, and it sings of Joy and peace and sings of dominion and authority and sings of prosperity and of restoration and healing. And I know He wrote it for me."

Katie stopped playing, placing the guitar on the floor beside her, but the sound still echoed within her heart, tears silent cascaded down her cheeks and she wondered, 'Lord, have I touched You too, have I ever touched You?'

She opened her eyes to see a verse on a page in her Bible she had highlighted years before.

I love those who love Me, and those who diligently seek Me - will find Me.

"What does that mean, what does that mean, we will find You? You didn't say I will reveal Myself to you, You said, you will find me, when you diligently seek Me?"

Katie lifted the page to her mouth and kissed The Word.

BREATH OF GOD

Suddenly and so unexpectedly she began sobbing as she thought of Adam, "You formed him out of the dust of the ground and breathed into his nostrils the breath of life... He became a living being. You kissed Him with the kisses of Your mouth. He was flooded with Your light and clothed in Your Glory."

You commanded the man,

> *You are free to eat from any tree in the garden, but you must not eat, from the tree of the knowledge of good and evil, for when you eat of it, you will surely die.*

He didn't believe You. Katie sobbed even harder as she could see played out before her eyes, the horror of what Adam's choice to disobey You, cost. Light congealed becomes blood.

It affected man and the earth; it touched everything and changed it to darkness and sorrow. Wars and sickness, death, poverty, every wickedness, violence. The wages of sin is death...

There was nothing mankind could do, nothing we could give, no price we could pay...

You taught Your people in love to offer lambs, goats, and bulls, but their blood could only cover sin, did not take it away. It could not clear the conscience, it could not draw us near to a Holy God, but You spoke, through Your prophets of The One who was to come.

And the Word became flesh and dwelt amongst us.
The very image of the invisible God.

> *Though He existed in very nature God, He did not consider equality with God, a thing to be grasped but emptied Himself, taking the nature of a servant and being made in human likeness. And found in appearance as a man, He humbled Himself, by becoming obedient to death, even death on a cross.*

Though Katie knew this, had heard it, read it, and knew it was the truth of the Christian faith; it was incredible, how even more real this had, just become to her. Is this the going deeper, is this the sweet revelation, is this the taste, and see? Katie pondered. It's sinking down.

> *For if the blood of goats and bulls and ashes of a heifer sprinkled on those who have been defiled, sanctify them; cleansing the flesh, making them outwardly clean, how much more will the Blood of Christ, who through the Eternal Spirit offered Himself without blemish to God, cleanse our consciences from dead works, to serve the Living God.*

> *The kindness and love of God appeared, He saved us, not because of righteous things we had done, not one of us but according to His mercy. He saved us by the washing of rebirth and renewal by the Holy Spirit, whom He poured upon us generously through Jesus Christ our Saviour.*

You said that

> "*You will die in your sins, if you do not believe that I am the One I claim to be, you will indeed die in your sins. I am, the Way, the Truth and the Life.*"

You said,

> "*You search the scriptures because you think that in them you have Eternal Life, it is these that testify of Me. And yet you are unwilling to come to Me so that you may have Life.*"

When Your people asked You,
"*What must we do, to do the works God requires?*"
You answered,

> "*The work of God is this; to Believe in the One He has sent.*"

Katie felt such a powerful anointing as she spoke the words. You laid down Your life, the Good Shepherd, the Lamb of God taking away the sin of the world, washed in Your Blood… Without the shedding of Blood there is no forgiveness. And You breathed on man and said, "Receive the Holy Spirit."

Katie fell face down on the bed and was so aware someone had walked in the room; she could not lift her head or turn her face to see. There was such a weighty presence and though it lasted what felt like seconds the fragrance that lingered remained for hours.

CHAPTER 3

If You Love Me

It was late and very dark as Katie reached for the bedside lamp, her whole day had been spent on her bed and now she had to stretch herself out and went to take a step and remembered her guitar on the carpet by her bed.

"You were here, weren't You, beautiful Lord?"

She went to the bathroom and had a hot shower, and a thought came to light candles and just enjoy Him more. She could play music softly, and read, it was another special day she did not want to end. Katie sat by candlelight and opened to the book of John, feeling led by His Spirit and there it was. Katie read it so softly, like a breathy whisper, so completely overwhelmed.

> *"On that day, you will realize I am in the Father, and you are in Me, and I am in you. Whoever has My commands and obeys them, he is the one who loves Me. He who loves Me will be loved by My Father, and I too will love him and reveal*

Myself to him… If anyone loves Me, he will obey My teaching, and My Father will love him, and We will come to him and make our home with him."

Katie felt such a prompt to head into Corinthians and opened to the scripture that was highlighted before her.

Do you not know that your body is a temple of the Holy Spirit, who is in you, whom you have received from God. You are not your own, you were bought at a price.

Katie raced through the pages until she came to the book of Peter, her eyes fell on the scripture,

Knowing that you were not redeemed with perishable things like silver or gold from your futile way of life inherited from your forefathers, but with the precious Blood as of a lamb, unblemished and spotless, the Blood of Christ… For He was foreknown before the foundation of the world but has appeared in these last times for the sake of you, who through Him, are believers in God, who raised Him from the dead and gave Him Glory, so that your faith and hope are in God.

GLORY AND HONOUR

"Oh Lord," Katie whispered, the intense leading of the Spirit was magnified, He was teaching and leading her, and she was desperate to follow, it almost felt like she was running as she flicked open the pages to Hebrews.

What is man that You are mindful of him, the son of man that You care for him? You made him a little lower than the angels;

You crowned him with Glory and honour and put everything under his feet.

In putting everything under him, God left nothing that is not subject to him, yet at present we do not see everything subject to him.

But we see, Jesus, who was made a little lower than the angels, now crowned with Glory and honour because He suffered death, so that by the grace of God He might taste death for everyone. In bringing many sons to Glory, it was fitting that God, for whom, and through whom, everything exists, should make the Author of their Salvation perfect through suffering.

All Katie heard was the word, "When?" it was an internal word, but so powerful. The Holy Spirit, her teacher was teaching her, as a Great Teacher does, he asks a question, thought provoking. So, she began reading the same passage again, to try and understand what He was revealing to her.

What is man that You are mindful of him, the son of man that You care for him? You made him a little lower than the angels; You crowned him with Glory and honour and put everything under his feet. And again, Katie heard the word, "When?"

"Oh Lord, David wrote it in the Psalms," Katie quickly found the scripture and read it aloud to the Lord.

"*When I consider Your heavens, the work of Your fingers, the moon, and the stars, which You have set in place. What is man that You are mindful of him, the son of man that You care for him? You made him a little lower than the heavenly beings and crowned him with Glory and honour. You made*

> *him ruler over the works of Your hands; You put everything under His feet."*

Katie heard the word again, "When?"

And then like an explosion inside her, she heard herself say, "In the garden, it was in the garden." Without hesitation, even though she knew what it said, she began reading right at the beginning, had to see it before her eyes.

Katie read aloud, the words from the book of Genesis.

"*Let us make man in our image*",

'Wow', she breathed,

> "*In our likeness, and let them rule over the fish of the sea and the birds of the air, over the livestock, over all the earth, and over all the creatures that move along the ground... So, God created man in His own image. In the image of God, He created him, male and female He created them.*"

God blessed them and said,

> "*Be fruitful and increase in number, fill the earth, and subdue it. Rule over the fish of the sea and the birds of the air and over every living creature that moves on the ground.*"

> *Then God said, "I give you every seed-bearing plant on the face of the whole earth and every tree that has fruit with seed in it. They will be yours for food. And to all the beasts of the earth and all the birds of the air and all the creatures that move on the ground-everything that has breath of life in it, I give every green plant for food."*

FALLING NAKED

When the woman saw that the fruit of the tree was good for food and pleasing to the eye, and desirable for gaining wisdom, she took some of it and ate it, she also gave some to her husband, who was with her, and he ate it. Then the eyes of both were opened, and they realized they were naked, so they sewed fig leaves together and made coverings for themselves. The Lord God called to the man, "Where are you?

"They were in the garden, in the cool of the day, hiding from You, among the trees." Katie relayed, "They were so afraid, because they knew they were naked, for the very first time. But You, Lord God made garments of skin for Adam and his wife and clothed them. Oh, the very weight of them, was so unlike the fig leaves, and nothing at all to be compared to the Glory that once clothed them."

And the Lord God said, *The man has now become like one of us, knowing good and evil. He must not, he must not be allowed to reach out his hand and take also from the tree of life and eat and live forever… So, the LORD God banished him from the garden of Eden, He drove the man out, He placed on each side of the garden of Eden cherubim and a flaming sword flashing back and forth to guard the way to the Tree of Life.*

CHAPTER 4

A New Wardrobe

Katie sat, just staring at the words, and felt such a heaviness upon her heart, and then, as only her Great Teacher could, He redirected her thoughts to a prophetic glimpse of Glory that was already in His heart. Before she even made it to the book of Isaiah she heard in her spirit,

> "Arise, shine for your light has come, and the Glory of the LORD rises upon you."
>
> *See darkness covers the earth and thick darkness is over the peoples, but the LORD rises upon you, and His Glory appears over you.*

Immediately she headed back to where she started in Hebrews, quickly her eyes focused on the Words.

> *But we see, Jesus, who was made a little lower than the angels, now crowned with Glory and honour because He suffered*

death, so that by the grace of God, He might taste death for everyone.

"In bringing many sons to Glory,"

Katie read it again.

"In bringing many sons to Glory."

The light of the candles was growing dim, her eyes were tired, but her spirit was awake. It was just after 3am but Katie was so deeply touched, like for the first time in the sweet revelation of what Christ had done. He had clothed those that were naked in His Righteousness, and a Garment of Salvation. We are not naked before You. He had restored the Glory and the honour upon us.

What if He did this to make the riches of His Glory known to the objects of His mercy, whom He prepared in advance for Glory – even us whom He also called not only from the Jews but also from the Gentiles, as He says in Hosea, I will call them My people who are not My people and I will call her My loved one, who is not My loved one.

"Good night, really it's good morning, my precious Lord and thank You, I am Your Loved one and You promise Your Beloved sweet sleep."

A NEW NAME

Katie loved prayer morning at the church, a small gathering of faithful, hungry ones lifting their voices in prayer and worship. They didn't just come and attend, they brought their hearts so open. They were the passionate seekers of the LORD, and the presence of God on those mornings was too beautiful to miss.

First there was time alone for the men to pray and meet with God, and then it was like the doors were flung wide open and the women and girls could come inside and pour their love, over the lover of their soul. Some of them fell to their knees, as they worshiped, some paced as they prayed. Katie loved to just sing, and used her arms as part of her dance, so adoring Him with her own expression. Katie loved to hear all the men and women pray so full of the Spirit. It was like each prayer was entwining and rising, as the room filled gloriously with more of His Presence.

Though they all prayed for revival, for souls for His Kingdom, and for the church and the community, it was always flooded with heart prayers for greater revelation of Him. And to love Him beyond what any of them had, to be truly so desperate, so hungry for Him.

He was the pursuit. With arms outstretched, He was the goal. Katie stood up as they closed in prayer and just felt so enveloped in love, if she didn't have work straight after she would stay in this place, it felt dreamy.

A man approached her and asked if he could speak to her a moment, Katie nodded. "Well, as I was praying, you came in my thoughts and the LORD said very clearly, "Tell her, Catherine is her name."

Katie was stunned, no one called her Catherine, though that is what her birth certificate read. It's like the name had been deleted, erased out, all her family and friends knew her, and called her, Katie. The man stood quietly and smiled as he spoke, "He said, He named you Catherine. That is what He calls you."

Katie felt the tears trickle down her cheeks at the very intimacy of His words. "Thank you," she said to the man as she turned to walk away.

The short drive home seemed like an eternity, as soon as she got in the door she put on the kettle and turned on her phone to look up the word Catherine. And there it was, 'Catherine' meaning 'Pure' and 'clean.'

"Glorious LORD thank You; this is what You named me, what You call me. Oh LORD thank You, with all my heart thank You."

A NEW SONG

Katie had such a lightness to her step, her thoughts continually on her LORD, the One who called her Catherine. She felt like a favoured daughter of her father. Like they shared something so intimate together that no one else knew, except the man whom the LORD had chosen to speak through.

The sun was shimmering on the tops of the water, at the river where Katie loved to walk. It didn't matter what time of day, if it was super early in the morning – during the day or late in the afternoon, or on rare occasions in the evenings with someone to walk with. This river walk was so beautiful.

Katie loved the pelicans the most, followed by the black swan, and the dolphins. She would often walk for an hour up and down the river path, patting all the dogs that were friendly, and just enjoying all 'the river family' as she called them.

She would sing to the LORD or chat away to Him about anything and everything, as she walked along. At times He would sing to her, but so often she would doubt. She would suddenly begin singing love songs that were all directed to her. He caused such joy to rise within her, even as she questioned," Is this really You?"

When Katie got home, she put the kettle on and felt such a prompt to turn her phone on and go to the keyboard, it was not words, simply an unction deep in her spirit.

Katie pressed record not knowing what to expect, but He is always faithful, and as soon as she began to play, a song that she didn't know came through her.

He sang to her; she merely played the chords, and He sang through her and to her.

My heart is open, step on in and dance with Me again, dance
with Me again, I love to twirl with you. I love the way you love
Me. I love the way you talk to Me; I love the way you show
Me every little thing, every little thing that amuses you.

I love the way you watch Me; I love the way you want Me
to see, what you see, but I say to you My child, I want you
to see what I see, what I see, when I look at you.
The depths of My heart when I look at you. I'm in love with you.
Truly I made you beautiful, truly I made you just like Me. I made
you glorious in My image. I made you according to My likeness
and I have drawn you; I've awakened you to Holy Love. Now take
it out, stand and sing, rise and shout it out, that I am your God.

I set you free, I delivered you. I have healed you, now the world
needs to know the Truth of who I am. I'm Alive, I am the Christ,
I am the Holy One. I am Gods Son; I am God's Son.

I love you; I love you; I love you; I breathe you
in, you breathe Me in, and we are One.

The tempo changed as He led her.

Higher, higher, higher, higher
Come with Me, come with Me, come away with Me.

I've got places you have never been, never seen. Come away with Me. Take My hand, I want to lead you higher. Love is beckoning you. There is no fear when you follow love, so come with Me. Rest your weary head upon My knee. I will touch your face so gently. I want to just look at you.

I want to see you resting. I want to see you filled with peace. I want to see you in the Secret Place, living in the Secret Place of My heart, always, never leave Me.

Oh, don't you know, that My heart breaks, every time you step away from My heart for you. Don't you know how I feel for you. I'm in love with your heart. I'm in love with your love for Me. I created you with passion. I created you to pour it all-over, all-over Me.

Stay with Me, stay with Me, stay with Me in the Secret Place, every moment, every moment, I love you."

Once again, the tempo shifted, though it was coming through her she was not creating it. Just merely allowing it to flow.

I will send you; I will take you; I will lead you. Just follow Me. Everywhere I go; you will be with Me, and everywhere you are, I will be with you, never alone, never alone.

Open your mouth and I will fill it; I will fill it.

The words are My words, My heart, My love for My Bride.
The words are My words – My love, for My Bride.
Can I use your mouth?
Can I use your heart?
Can I use you, My daughter, My love?

Yes, LORD use me, yes LORD take me, walking and dancing on streets of gold. Show me Your face, my heart cries out to You, Your face, Your face, Your face, Your face.

I want to see You with my eyes, my heart, my heart cries show me, show me Your face.

I'm so caught up in seeing You, it's all I want, I want to see You and breathe You. I want to be clothed with You, I want to wear You, and walk with You, and dance with You. I want to just run in freedom. Let freedoms song flow with me, I want the world to see You – when they look at me.

Katie, remained quiet, He had finished, and she sat overwhelmed and so grateful for the prompt to turn on her phone and record. She made a coffee in a takeaway cup and headed out the door. The song when played through the car speakers would be so much better and the drive to the hills, would be the place to hear it. But she just knew that she had to hear His Words again, and again, and again. And to try with all her heart not to doubt that it was Him.

CHAPTER 5

Joy Unspeakable

Katie woke before the dawn and felt a moist spot on her chin, she was dribbling, with a huge grin on her face. It was like she had spent the night hearing the most wonderful, delightful news, as if someone had shared a story all night long as she slept.

She was excited and it beamed through her, her smile like a bride on her wedding day, but she could remember none of it, only the immense pleasure it had brought her soul. She made her way to the kitchen and put on the kettle and made a coffee to take outside to her prayer chair, (swing seat) in her back yard.

The sky was so full of stars it was heavenly to behold the beauty. She tried to trace back in her mind but all she got was joy, and the more she thought about it, the larger her smile seemed to grow. It wasn't laugh out loud, it was deep and full and unspeakable like Peter had shared, only she had no idea why. She sat there swinging on her chair, grinning, and pondering as the sun came out. As beautiful as it was, Katie questioned, There has got to be more than this? As disappointment climbed in.

How quickly it changed to tears as she recalled in her mind the things her friends had shared with her and the experiences they were having. She knew not to compare, but it started rising within her. Then the most powerful gush of love and joy flooded her heart and soul, as the words came boldly into her mind.

"The Kingdom of God is Righteousness," and it was like a solid clicking into place of the breastplate, completely covering her heart and lungs and vital organs.

"It is Peace," and Katie experienced the overwhelming velvety blanketing Peace as it flooded her heart and mind. It felt like being tucked in, safe and secure.

"It is Joy," It is Joy in the Holy Spirit. Joy unspeakable, The Joy of the Lord is your strength. Katie could not silence the roar of laughter that came through her. Each time she thought it had finished; another burst of Joy would be released. It changed to a childlike giggle, as she sat with The One, she could not see, so happy, so clothed, complete, lacking nothing. Anyone looking on would have thought she had drunk too much wine, even at this hour of the morning. Katie felt giggly, girly, and free.

"In Your very presence is the fullness of Joy," Katie proclaimed. "I love Your Presence."

THE STONE

On the seventh ring, Shelley picked up her phone, saying "Hello Katie, how are you?"

"Shelley, do you have time to talk?"

"Sure, are you ok?"

"Do you remember that day at the Light House?"

"You mean the day of the angel?" Shelley asked with humour in her voice.

There was a long silence and Shelley inquired, "Are you there, we seem to have bad reception?"

"I'm just driving," Katie said making a quick excuse. "Shelley, do you remember what it was about?"

"Well, you said you were casting your cares, and a little girl came and sat with you, and wanted the stone, yeah, that's right, and she left with it."

"Only you said she wasn't a little girl, but a messenger an angel?" Katie added.

"Because the care wasn't a care at all, but just your perspective of it!" Shelley added amazed at her own recollections of that day. "So why do you ask about it now?"

Another long silence, and then with a quavering voice she stammered, "Because the stone turned up on my prayer chair today." Katie did not feel to share that she noticed it at the very moment she had sat smiling and laughing, flooded with His joy.

"Whoa, that's incredible, are you sure it's the same stone?"

"It was smooth and oval, it was white with flecks of grey and black, it's like I was meant to notice and remember it, that day, for some reason, before I handed it to her."

"Where is it now?" Shelley asked with much excitement in her voice.

"It's in my pocket." Katie shared through smiling lips. It was like a mysterious treasure, not because it was a stone but because of the journey it had been on since it had passed from her hand to the hand of the angel.

"So, God has done all this to get your attention, is there something He was getting you to look at?" Shelley questioned.

Katie chose to remain silent.

"Well, was He asking you to go overseas, you know like missions?"

"No not like that..." Katie interrupted.

Well, has He found you a man to marry?"

"No, not like that..."

"But He has asked you something, to do something or,"

"Yes," Katie started to cry, "I have not wanted to ignore it, Him, but I'm, afraid..."

Shelley broke through the sound of her sobs and said, "He loves you; do you know that?"

"He flooded me with so much joy today; I laughed and laughed with Him. I know that! His presence is so real to me." Katie cried.

"Are you really driving?" Shelley queried.

"Yes, I'm heading out to The Light House."

"Would you like me to meet you there; we could pray together?"

"Actually, I might just go to the park that's near there and sit on the swings and look out to the water, and..."

"I'm only a phone call away, He loves you, remember, He wouldn't ask you to do something, if He didn't think you could. He must trust you."

MY SWEET LADY

Katie was so thankful there were no children on the swings or playing in the park, though there were families sitting on picnic rugs by the river.

Just being alone with Him was lovely but like in any relationship she needed to talk about what was on His heart, and as much as she loved Him, she was afraid. He is the One who holds the whole universe in the span of His hands. She had put it off and tried to ignore and He had gently been persistent in wanting her to answer Him.

Even though she had walked with Him for years, this was different. All the love, the joy, the peace, were just the beginnings of what He was inviting her into, the depths of His heart. The deep meaning behind the joy she woke in, He had been sharing His heart with her awakened heart, she knew it. Only love could bring this much joy. His Love, His Holy Love. Katie prayed in the Spirit, so unsure of what to say to Him, even though she knew, He knew her every thought, there was nothing she could hide from Him. A song suddenly rose up in her heart, and before she realised what she was doing, she began singing.

"Lady, my sweet lady," then suddenly it burst out of her mouth, "Is that You, LORD?"

"I'm as close as I can be." She cut off the song by questioning again, "Is that You, LORD, is that You?"

Her mind, her thoughts recalling all the times He had prompted her to turn on her phone and record the songs. All the time, friends had sat with her as she sang and they wept, and sharing when she had stopped, that it was 100%, it was exactly what the person had been sharing privately with the LORD, and what He had been revealing to them.

"Oh, why LORD, do I find it so hard to believe, that the God who created everything, would sing absolutely beautiful love songs to me?"

Katie jumped off the swing and went for a run along the river, but she could not run fast enough to get away from the question. Why she found it so very hard to believe? Doubts were larger in her mind than faith. Why was this her stumbling block? She believed when others spoke and sang The Father's heart, why did she struggle repeatedly in this area? This place of intimacy.

All those years ago He had spoken to her at the kitchen table, and He said the words 'you're an incubator of intimacy' and though she knew He was describing her, still she replied, 'That's not even scriptural.'

"Is it that I just don't trust You?" But as soon as the words were out of her mouth, she knew that was not the truth.

"Is it that I can't believe that You could love me, not just through the cross revealing Your great love for all the world. Lord, is it because I have so much trouble believing You love me?" Tears sprang up from the depths of her heart. "That I uniquely, personally matter, like -" and then the flood gates opened. "Like when I was married and oh so loved, like that You could love me, even deeper than he did, and You really want too, and You want me to believe it."

Katie lay on the grass in the sun; sobbing, crying hurt, it came from so deep, but she knew He had helped her find the truth in love and patience. Tenderly with the Holy Spirit guiding her, He wanted this revealed, He wanted her free to receive His Love.

How tender is it, that a man would go to the cross for us, to wash us clean of all our sin, not just any man, the only man who could. And how tender is it, that this same man would continue to pursue us. "Oh Lord, help me, to really believe this is You, I pray."

With that Katie made her way back to her car and headed home, she remained silent as the words of the song played over in her mind.

CHAPTER 6

The Invitation

Katie woke but not in the overflowing joy of yesterday, she felt different, something had shifted from her heart, peace and such a cosy feeling was all she could understand. She enjoyed her river walk and patting all the dogs along the path, it was such a lovely time of day just after 5am, crispness in the air, it always surprised her how many walked so early. All the people seemed so friendly in the morning.

She arrived home quickly to feed her cat then raced off to the church prayer meeting. The cosy feeling remained, as they all prayed and sang it was like a feeling of coming home. All the prayer points lifted to The One who hears, and though Katie loved to pray she never prayed except in the Spirit, but without a doubt she knew He wanted her there, so in obedience and love of His presence – she came.

Lisa a lady she had met briefly touched her arm gently as the prayer wound up for the morning.

"Katie, how glorious is our God!" Katie noticed it was like she just breathed Him in as she spoke.

"God has placed upon my heart to invite Glory women to a prayer gathering at a friend's place, just in this area, it will be tonight at 7pm. He asks you to come, He wants you to come, there will only be a small group of us. This is the address," she said as she handed Katie a note. "I have to head off now to get the kids ready for school, have a great day, hope we see you there."

NOT AFRAID

It was such a busy morning at work, at times it felt like she was running trying to get all the things done. But she thrived on being productive, and customer service was her sweet spot, whether behind the counter or out on the floor. Every customer was her favourite, and it brought her so much joy going the extra mile for all of them.

Just after 2pm, it quietened down and she had time to really get a good clean up done; picking up clothes and rehanging them, dusting shelves, creating the standard her boss loved – excellence, and the reason all the customers kept coming back. As she worked her mind pondered the women of the Bible, it really amazed her none of them seemed intimidated by Him, and she began enjoying an internal conversation with Him.

They weren't afraid to come to You, were they? Like the Syrophoenician woman, she came running out to you bowing down before You and calling "Lord, son of David." Your disciples were intent on sending her away, and even You said, "I was only sent to the lost sheep of Israel." She begged You to help, not for herself but for her daughter. Did that give her greater courage, I wonder. You said, *"It's not good to take the children's bread and toss it to the dogs,"* she wasn't offended as so many of us would have been. She responded, *"Yes Lord, but even the dogs eat the crumbs that fall from the masters table."* And You answered, *"O woman, great is your faith, let it be done for you as you desire."* Her daughter was healed at once.

What about the woman with the issue of blood, she wasn't afraid to be out in the crowd, though by law she shouldn't have been. She was considered unclean, but what is more, she knew something about You, not just that You were a rabbi, a teacher or a healer. She was not intimidated to come after You in a crowd and reach for the hem of Your garment. She had spent all she had on physicians and could not be healed by any, but she came from behind You and touched You, for she had said to herself, *"If only I touch His garment, I shall be made well."* Immediately she felt the blood dry up, she knew she was healed of her affliction. But You turned around, You felt power had gone out from You and You were asking, *"Who touched Me?"* The woman came and fell before You, fearing and trembling and she came and told You the truth. She was in a crowd of people who all knew the law, she would not have known what You were going to say, she only knew what she felt. She felt the power that had gone out from You, a power she had never experienced before, had gone into her. And You said, *"Daughter your faith has made you well, go in peace."* I wish in that moment The Word of God captured the face of God.

What about Mary and Martha, they weren't afraid to have You in their home, they weren't hiding in their rooms because of what they had come to know about You. Martha cooked for You, she even came right up to You and said, "Lord, do You not care that my sister has left me to serve all alone." She could have said that to her brother Lazarus, but she was comfortable with You, You loved them she knew it. It's too incredible but You were their friend. Or did she lose sight of the magnitude of who You were because You looked like a man? Mary sat near You and listened to You. And when their brother died both came out to You, at separate times, both with the same heart full of grief, Saying, *"Lord if You had of been here my brother would not have died."* We know that Martha said to You, *"I believe You are the Christ, the Son of God, even He who comes into the world."* She was standing face to face with You when she said those words. *"You are the Christ, the Son of God."* Both sisters saw You raise their brother; You revealed Yourself more and more to them.

You said to Martha in a hidden conversation, *"Did I not say to you that if you believe you will see the Glory of God."* Mary even took a pound of very costly perfume, pure nard and anointed Your feet and wiped them with her hair, she wasn't afraid to be so close to You. So close. And when the disciples criticised her, You defended her; just as You did when Martha complained to You, against her. You said, *"Let her alone, why do you bother her? She has done a good deed to Me. For you will always have the poor with you, but whenever you desire you can do good to them, but you do not always have Me. She has done what she could; she has anointed My body beforehand for burial. Truly I say to you, wherever the gospel is preached in the whole world, what this woman has done will also be spoken of."*

Not only was she not afraid of You, but this gesture, of her 'scented love,' that You would never forget and nor would You allow any of us too, was the very fragrance, when You were stripped of everything. It was the only thing that remained.

What about Mary Magdalene, it was her that loved much, wasn't it? That came into the house of the Pharisee with her alabaster jar of fragrant oil and stood at Your feet behind You, weeping and washing Your feet with her tears, and wiping them with the hair of her head, and she kissed Your feet and anointed them. She knew something about You, that it moved her to come where she wasn't welcome. Just to be at Your feet, You said, *"Her sins which are many, are forgiven, because she loved - much."* It was this same Mary, who loved much that You first appeared to in a garden, when you revealed Yourself alive to her after being laid in a tomb. Even then when

You spoke her name, *"Mary,"* as she was beholding You and wanting to cling to You, this same Mary who had been at Your cross and watched and listened as You died. How can it be- that even in this, after You were raised to life, she was not afraid of You? The very enormity of who You really are. The Word of God, Abraham's friend, The King of Glory, From everlasting to everlasting, the Living GOD.

"Oh Jesus," Katie whispered, "Oh Jesus!"

THE GIFT

At ten to seven, Katie pulled up to the address written on the note of paper that had been handed to her that morning. Many times, she wondered should she go but here she was parked on the road outside of a home of people she didn't really know. As she walked toward the front door, she could hear worship music playing and people talking. She knocked on the door and a lady she had never met greeted her, but she smiled with such warmth that it felt welcoming.

"Another Glory worshiper, welcome, I'm Jodie, come on through." Katie followed as they walked through the home and tried to take in all the glorious paintings on the walls. It was prophetic and if she had time, she would love to know the meaning behind them all. But the picture that grabbed her attention, was one of a Light House. Just as she entered the lounge room, Katie was so pleased to see the familiar face of the lady from the prayer meeting, even though truthfully, she didn't know her name.

Like reading her mind, the lady stepped forward with a hand of greeting, "Hi we haven't been officially introduced, I'm Lisa." Then all the introductions followed as they each found a place to sit on cushions or lounge chairs or to stand. The music was turned off, and Jodie picked up a guitar and led them all into a deep place of worship. It took no longer than a few minutes and they all came to the carpet due to the weighty presence. They laid in the silence with the occasional, "Holy" released from an overflowing response of awe. It was wonderful, there was so very little prayer, and yet it felt like they had accomplished something great just coming together and allowing Him to move. It felt like moments, but hours had passed in that atmosphere, no one wanted to leave but slowly they all stood to their feet.

Jodie was wearing a beautiful smile as she turned to Katie and said, "I have something for you, wait here." She disappeared into another room and came back with a package wrapped loosely in tissue paper. She then handed it to her. "He told me to buy this months ago and have this written on it, I never understood why, I only found out tonight as we lay on the floor who He wanted me to give if too." Katie was thankful there was no sticky tape as she opened the bundle, she gasped… There was two towels one blue, one pink, and the pink one read, "*Lady*" Katie felt like hugging it to herself as she wondered what was written on the other. And as she lifted the top towel, there it was "*Lord*."

And suddenly the words of the song penetrated her heart, and she heard it deep within, "Lady, my sweet Lady, I'm as close as I can be." Goose bumps went all over her entire body. "I can see that this means something very significant to you." Jodie smiled so delighted to have been used by The Lord and seeing it confirmed before her eyes. Katie thanked her so very much and said her goodbyes to all those there and headed to her car. As soon as she turned the corner she squealed with delight.

"You love me, and You sing to me."
All the way home Katie sang the words of the
song and sang to Him her own song,
"I believe You, I believe You, I am Yours and You
are mine and You deeply love me."

The car itself filled with such a lovely fragrance, and she knew without doubt it was Him.

As she lay her head on the pillow that night, she heard the scripture from deep within her. *We have come to know and have Believed the love which God has for us.* Katie smiled. "I know and Believe!" Katie confessed with such a revelation. *God is love, and the one who abides in love abides in God and God abides in him.*

CHAPTER 7

Waves Of Love

Katie had stopped watching TV years ago, it happened in a time of deep sorrow, when even the tissue adds of little ducklings walking across the screen made her cry. She never missed watching TV at all, but she borrowed the occasional movie from the library, yet more and more she felt to let go of that indulgence to keep her mind on Him.

But the other night laying on her bed she flicked through her phone and was so excited because Holy Spirit fires were breaking out all over the world. It was like it was magnified before her eyes. In those very places where the people had gone too far, too blinded, and too consumed in the lusts of the flesh. It wasn't just one country, it was in all, and He was using men and woman and children out on the streets not afraid of the Gospel, preaching and praying and loving those in the dark.

Crowds humbly coming to the call, and falling on their knees weeping, repenting, being set free and delivered. It wasn't legalistic and religious; they heard the message and were moved by His Spirit. They had been rescued from the domain of darkness and translated into the Kingdom of His Beloved Son.

God's heart is that none would be lost, and waves and waves and waves of His love washed across the hearts of man and flooding dry and thirsty lands. It was happening on beach fronts and esplanades, in town squares, along highways as they marched with banners lifting the Name JESUS and shouting out His praise.

Some friends continued to send her links of all the evil, the wickedness that truly was taking place around the world. But He made it so clear to her, 'to keep her eyes on Him.' It was like He was keeping her focus on what He was doing, not on the work of the evil one. All Katie could see was Paul's words to the Colossians. All over the world this gospel is bearing fruit and growing, just as it has been doing among you since the day you heard and understood God's Grace in all its Truth.

"Now, how can I sleep?" Katie asked, "with all this going on, Your children all around the world have been humbling themselves and seeking Your face, and turning from their wicked ways, praying and their heart cry, there constant heart cry was always Revival and You are moving, thank You precious Lord."

Katie turned on her bedside lamp and opened her Bible, "Lord, this prayer is for all of us across the nations, ones that are yours now and those that are coming in on the waves of Your Glory and Love.

> *For this reason, since the day we heard of it, we have not ceased to pray for you and to ask that you may be filled with the knowledge of His Will in all spiritual Wisdom and Understanding – so that you will walk…"*

Katie sat up in bed,

> *"In a manner worthy of The Lord, to please Him in all respects, bearing fruit in every good work and increasing in the knowledge of God – strengthened with all Power, according to His glorious Might, for the attaining of all steadfastness and patience; Joyously giving thanks. Yes Lord! Joyously giving thanks to the Father, who has qualified us to share in the inheritance of the saints in Light."*

CUP OF LOVE

Katie sat in a candle lit room and just talked to her LORD, with intimate music softly playing.

"Do You know how I see You?" she asked smiling. "Do You understand how I enjoy You? Do You realize I'm drawn to Your gentleness? David said, 'It makes us great.' I love the poetry of You. I remember the day all those years ago when I discovered that You are a poet as I read the book of Malachi, and over and over and over, I repeated it to You, oh God You're a poet, You're a poet and in that moment there was nothing more beautiful because You gave me a love of words, Your words. You captivated me; I could not resist You.

I love the colours and the landscape you created; I love all the sounds, the perfumes, and the beauty. And I love the seasons, and You know spring has remained my favourite, what's Yours I wonder? I love every word that was spoken through Your mouth from Your heart. I love that Your lips are anointed with grace. I love that You kiss us with the kisses of Your mouth. I love that You created us in Your image.

I love that You make us believe that we as mere man could really come to know You, God, not just a word on a page, or a statement of fact, like it says this, so that's it! No! You invite us to come – You welcome us to search for You like a lost treasure."

Though Katie was still smiling silent tears of love flowed, she loved this quiet place of just talking to Him, not asking for anything. "You want us to discover You, tear the wrappings off and really look at You." Katie wiped at the tears that were running down her cheeks and was reminded of David saying how, *You collected all my tears in Your bottle, You have recorded each one in Your book.*

You want to live in us, fill us with all that You are, that we lack no good thing. I love that You are a Love God, it's who You are, I love that You are Spirit, and that Spirit is Holy. I love that You are Light, and in You there is no darkness. You light me up and cause me to shine.

I love that I delight in You in the simple things like candlelight or waking early on a winters morning just to see Your stars that You know each by name, You set them in place. It reminds me of Your conversation with Abraham, where You took him outside and You said,

> *Look up at the heavens and tell the stars if indeed you can count them, so shall your descendants be.*

I don't believe there was ever a night as clear as that one, to reveal the wonder of Your Grand promise.

I love that You listen, You never leave, I love that You care, I love that You know me and really want to. I love that You never ask me to go for a walk - away from You. I love that You created us for family, for relationships but I love that you waited so patiently for me to love just being with You and that it's all right with You that I'm so content with You alone. Walking and driving, everything I do, dancing, You complete me.

I love that You are brilliant, You are Wisdom, that You know the answer to everything, I love that You teach us. I love that You are patient, I love that when You found us and drew us to Yourself, we were babies, born again new creations that needed milk and the gentleness of a loving Father.

I love that You are never afraid, I really love that You are never afraid, and that You don't worry about anything, that You are confidence and strength. I love that I know I need You.

I love trying to surprise You, like when I use to buy big bunches of lilies and roses and pretend, they weren't for You at the florist and then I would lay them on the altar at a church just to bless You. I love that You always showed me who You wanted them given too... because You really care about all the hidden pain Your children go through and You showed them, "I see you."

In my mind I'm nestled in against You, I'm hiding under Your wings, I'm standing in Your shadow, and Your love is raining down around me, Your joy is all abounding, and I am free because You are in me. Wow, do You remember when You gave me this song? It feels like a lifetime ago, on a verandah in another home, on my prayer chair.

How little did I know then that the storm would escalate, it wasn't just winds and rain. This was a hurricane and if not for Your hand I would have just been blown away. Sometimes I wanted too.

I love You God.

We call it a hunger and a thirst, we call it surrender, we call it so many things. We want to linger in Your presence like Joshua did in the tent of meeting. We want to want; what You want us to want - to desire. How much we must fall short of what You have, to share with us.

I love waking up and being so aware of You, I love being overly sentimental not wanting to close my eyes and go to sleep, not wanting to miss a thing. But I love that even when I sleep my heart remains awake to listen to You as You rejoice over me with singing.

I love the thought of waking to hear You. I love that I cannot live without You. I love that You are passionate and that You're jealous over me. I love that You smile within me. I love that I have a secret smile just for You. I love that You are funny, gentle, and powerful, and that You're my anchor.

I love that I really like You, there is none that compare with You, none could take Your place.

I love that You took me by Your righteous right hand, I love that You have taken my right hand, I love that it means we are face to face – every step.

I Love most of all that You gave us this cup, it's something solid to hold onto when everything else has been stripped away and the bread to eat, that I have wept all over as I come closer to You than to anyone else in the world.

I love that You said that You are the Living Bread that came down from heaven to give Your life to the world.

You said,

> *Except you eat of My flesh and drink My Blood you have no life in you. And whoever eats My flesh and drinks My Blood abides in Me and I in him.* And then You said *If you abide in Me and My words abide in you, you can Ask whatever you desire, it will be given you. This is too My Fathers Glory that you bear much fruit, showing yourselves to be My disciples.*

You said,

Remember Me, remember My death until I come.

You said,

My Words are Spirit – My Words are Life.

This covenant is cut with My Blood.

With closed eyes, Katie sat cross legged on the carpet with The Lord of All as she ate of His flesh and drank His Blood.

I can never say to You, that I can't come close enough because You came all the way from heaven to fill every part of me.

THE SMILE OF LOVE

Julie a long-time friend of Katie's came after work every Tuesday, it was usually with another friend Libby, and they all made dinner together and shared their week, prayed and played games or read the bible, it was always different, they even painted. Sometimes they cried and held each other, sometimes they laughed, they simply enjoyed each other's company.

Over the last fortnight Libby had been involved in meetings on the Tuesday with her new church. Julie and Katie really started to share about the things God had placed upon their hearts. They finished their meal which was always delicious and sat in the lounge room, Julie chose the carpet with pillows, and a minky blanket and Katie took up her favourite position on the lounge. She turned the CD player on and suddenly they found themselves talking about personal things from their lives, that very few people knew about. As Katie began to share, she found it a struggle because the memories of the day were locked away in deep regret. They asked Holy Spirit to lead, guide and to encourage truth in their memories. Katie closed her eyes and allowed herself to remember the significant parts of that day. And with open trust of her friend, she began to share.

"This all happened many years ago. Finally, Cassie and Bek, friends I dearly love, were able to step away from their busy schedules and meet with me at the park, you know the one by the river near here? We, all walked to the fish and chip shop and ordered takeaway. We were so delighted to just be in each other's company. We laughed and they shared what they had been doing, the places they had gone, the new levels of Glory they were entering. It was all so exciting; they both had many spiritual encounters;

they both saw into the spirit realm and would often try to describe what they had seen to me. As we made our way to an uprooted tree, we all found places to sit on it, it was very close to the water. It was a beautiful sunny day clear skies, the temperature was perfect.

Cassie noticed a man who was walking through the park, stopping to talk to a few people. She kept pointing out his smile, Bek and I turned and looked at him briefly. I was more caught up in feeding the pelicans that had swam over, it brought me so much joy, they are still my favourites. Cassie kept on about the man that had gone to sit on the swings smiling, she couldn't take her eyes off him. She was amazed that a man of that age would be so comfortable walking alone through the park and to even sit on a swing smiling. After a while he got off the swing and walked in the direction of the Jetty at the other end of the park.

When we made it back home for a cup of coffee, we all reflected on the people in the park. We all felt like we had missed something, did someone need prayer? One question led to another, and it all stopped as Cassie brought up the man again, there was something about him, a man of his age alone walking through a park and sitting on the swings watching everyone and smiling. Next minute one of them blurted out, "Was he an angel?" No sooner than the question came another question followed "Was he a Holy man?" It stunned me how quickly they were both picking up things in the spirit, about who this man could be.

The conversation seemed to last for hours, and most of it in regret for missing him, Cassie not walking over to him, or why he didn't come to talk with them, even though Cassie noticed he smiled at them and quite contentedly watched them.

It really made me look at the afternoon in a different light. I had barely given the man a second glance even though Cassie never stopped talking about his beautiful smile. I was disappointed in myself for not taking notice as I was so happy just being with my friends and watching the pelicans. I had observed him so little to see he was wearing blue, that's all I could remember, I think he wore a cap. Bek had looked at him, but her attention was truly on other things as well, it wasn't until we all began talking that she really came to realise that perhaps there was something more about this man.

Cassie was the one to say what they were all beginning to imagine, "Was it the Lord?" with that she got such a jolt in the spirit. Cassie could not understand what kept her from doing what she would normally do and that would be to walk over and talk to the person. All three of us pondered and questioned ourselves and were discouraged with the lack of recognition of such an encounter.

Cassie was closer, her position on the tree trunk had her facing that way toward the man. The man almost mesmerized her; she was drawn to his smile. I was so jealous, why didn't I face that way, even to look at his smile. To really notice him. I found myself as did the others questioning our walk with Him. It felt like it was the measure of the relationship we each had with Him, and mine was the very least and it deeply saddened me, all because of a day at the park I had been so happy in the moment I never saw Him enter it."

Katie opened her eyes, her heart laid bare, the deep regret and disappointment right at the surface.

"Katie" Julie spoke, "Katie, do you know what I picked up as you shared? Condemnation and guilt that you need to be set free of. I don't know if the man was The Lord, but either way you've already said, he was smiling. He was happy watching you all, enjoying you all, His children in the place he created.

You didn't all miss it. Wow! The condemnation you must have all walked in, instead of the memory of a beautiful day. Which he delighted in, and you know that because he was smiling watching you all. You were just being you; it's time to enjoy that He did come to be with you all. Not to talk to you all, but to enjoy you just being yourselves.

The one who continued to look at him was more interested in the man for whatever reason, she is an evangelist, or simply just enjoyed observing people. The other lady had other things on her heart that day, like just sitting with you and watching you feed the pelicans. If He had wanted you all to know, He would have – you would not have had to come home and process, it would have been so clear. And another thing, the ridiculous scale you placed upon yourself, believing that how much you were looking at Him revealed the measure of your relationship with him. Garbage! That you were the least. Absolute lies! Katie, you love Him, and your love for Him is not in competition with another or what they have done or where they have gone in ministry for Him.

I, say this to you as a friend, it's time to repent, change the way you think. And whether you believe it was Him or not, truly I don't think that really matters, but being free of the condemnation and guilt and the lies that's what really matters. And to remember that special day you had with your friends you had not seen for so long."

A weight lifted off Katie's heart as she repented aloud and she smiled with great delight, for the new way she could see the past.

CHAPTER 8

Come And See This

Friday was a special day in Katie's week, she met in her home with a special friend, and they just welcomed God... Every week was so different, they often laughed and laughed without reason, they prayed, they danced, they played and sang, and with the precious Holy Spirit, they were moved and though they didn't always understand, they always cherished their night.

They would have a pretty platter of cheeses, crackers and grapes, bananas, blueberries, dark chocolate all set up on the coffee table, in the lounge room... lots of candles and music. Both admitted it was a very special highlight to their week and though they could go anywhere on a Friday night this was everything, just to be in His Glory Presence, together.

He had caused them to meet years ago, and though they had a few phone calls which were heavenly and met up occasionally, it was now in this season, that He had drawn them both, for His timing and purpose. And both loved and valued it. And though it was always fun and playful, they both knew each week they were being set free of more and learning how to stay in His Joy. As they came together, they would share the places they still needed to lean into God more, to yield and repent. They kept each other accountable and encouraged each other.

After the last night with Him, they both spoke about what they could remember they did in His Presence for seven hours. It shocked them, normally they could say, we played the keyboard and sang, or we painted, or we read or whatever it was, even though they never planned anything, but they could not really recall all that had taken place.

This last Friday night was so different, they didn't do a lot of worship, either singing or playing keyboard or guitars, they didn't read, much. They were never bored or wondered what we shall do now, it just flowed. His Presence was so strong and at midnight when her friend was about to leave the Presence of God intensified, and they both knew He was not finished with them yet. They stood in front of a homemade poster of Revival, and they were moved by the Spirit powerfully, there was some words but mostly sounds and languages that God had blessed them with. There are no words to describe the dance and the prayer, they just knew they were interceding and being used by God above and beyond what the mind could understand.

And then just as suddenly the intensity shifted, and they were saturated with enormous peace. Katie like a child asked to see His Glory cloud. As her friend wandered out to her car, to pack her things she had brought with her, she quickly raced back in the front door. "Come and see this." She had such awe and excitement in her voice.

Katie walked out to the driveway and tried to suppress her laughter, she could barely see the street, the houses, or the cars. The longer they stood out on the street watching and trying not to laugh the thicker the cloud or mist got. It was noticeable because of the streetlights. They had to go back in the house to laugh out loud, it may have been just a coincidence, but it was huge, they had no answer for it, and nor were they looking for one. But they did wonder was He smiling with them, very aware of their thoughts and the delight it brought them.

ITS TIME TO LET GO

Katie woke happy, she knew something powerful had taken place last night. She was well pleased they had been led to pray for Revival just before midnight, but there was something else going on inside of her. Her special friend and her grandson had breakfast with her. Katie then played the keyboard and sang, and a thought came to her mind about the Teddies. Katie walked alone into her bedroom without saying a word, opened the cupboard doors and reached up to take hold of Penny the Penguin and two Teddy bears and looked at the white Teddy on her bed.

All those years ago when her husband had died, a friend had asked the Lord, "What shall I get her?" He had replied, "A Teddy Bear" but she did not believe so she brought roses, and again He impressed on her heart "To buy her a Teddy Bear." The roses died, which brought more death around her, but in her arms every night was a brown Teddy Bear. Unfortunately, she was not alone in the comfort the Teddy brought, as her cat would continuously knead the Teddy tummy throughout the night until the fur was nearly gone. Eventually Katie brought another soft toy it was Penny the Penguin, who at one stage had a roundish look, but once again she shared it with the cat, it became very flat.

When that cat died a friend made a very special memorial Teddy with his name on it. She couldn't think to bring herself to have it in the bed with her, so it remained in the top of the cupboard alongside the original brown Teddy. Penny the Penguin was looking shabby over the years, so Katie bought a white Teddy Bear, Penny was placed up in the cupboard with the other two. And then her elderly cat died and though she bought a rescue cat, she still missed her cat as only the Lord knew to the extent.

So since then, every night Katie lay in bed her arms wrapped around her white Teddy. And now she picked it up off the bed. All these Teddies had been a place of comfort, and though they had no soul she certainly did, she needed to be free of the past, and all the tears and all the memories, all the grief all the emotions associated with the Teddies. Katie had even taken the brown bear on a three-day camping holiday as she was so used to sleeping with a bear, it had become normal.

She carried them out of the room and her friend's young grandson saw them and wanted them, but Katie knew she could buy him other Teddy Bears but these she had to get rid of. Katie walked with such determination, and one by one placed them in the bin for the council collection the following Tuesday.

Only The LORD could have brought her so much peace and prepared her heart, so she could truly know it was time to let go. No tears, no pain, no sorrow. And no regrets. It was time to give Him that place to really comfort her, His arms always waiting.

Both Katie and her friend were surprised by what He had begun in them with clearing things out of their homes, books, their brand-new clothes and shoes, items from kitchen cupboards and drawers, even their hearts, and minds. In all these special nights of coming together, He really was moving, and it was inside of them. He was changing them, and they so welcomed it.

SOME MEMORIES ARE WORTH HOLDING ONTO

Katie was 3 days into her fast and for some reason she felt flat and emotional and yet this last while had been one of great joy.

Katie read the beginnings of the prophets Isaiah and Jeremiah and prayed, her morning had been lovely, and the river walk so was special meeting new people, but there was something that made her feel almost like tears. She experienced the slightest impression to go through her work she had done all those years ago. She had a binder full of pages that she had written, they were all about what The Word of God meant to her personally.

All those years ago, some in the class had completed at least five scriptures a week, not Katie, she would read it and then go to the park near her home and listen to worship music and sing her heart out. Every day when she had the opportunity, she would return to the park with worship music and focus on that one scripture for the week.

It brought to mind that day she was in playful mood and did not know what CD to pack in her pink bag with her Walkman. So, she grabbed one CD after another until she had maybe 20 in her bag, as she was heading out the front door, she heard a voice inside of her asking, "How long are we going, a week?" Katie started laughing and then all the way running to the park she laughed, saying "Is that You Holy Spirit, it's You, isn't it?" Laughing so uncontrollably and all these years later the words He spoke still made her laugh.

But on that particular day, years ago, it was not at the park she found understanding of the week's scripture verse. Church had finished and as always everyone went into the café for coffee and cakes and fellowship. Katie loved to have the whole church to herself, and she would make her way to the front with her Walkman and her favourite CD, it was like when she put the plugs in her ears, she blocked out everything else and she danced and danced in so much joy. His presence lingered from all the corporate worship but something amazing happened and she lost track of time just dancing and singing. One of the ladies who ran the café called out to her, and she was so stunned, they were closing the doors, everyone had gone. She had been there that long!

Katie remembered that day coming into her home before her world turned on its axis. Her beloved was downstairs watching TV. She said her hellos and went upstairs to cook. Later, out to her verandah and listen to her CD, but she was drawn back inside to the loungeroom and looked at her verse which read, *I am complete in Him.* She had the Walkman tucked into her clothes and picked up her pen and notepad and began to write.

I am wallpapering the insides of my heart with Your words of love – Jer 31:3

> *I have loved you with an everlasting love, I have drawn you with loving kindness.*

Your words have me feeling intoxicated each time I speak them out. I am filled with another burst of Your Joy, I am giddy and girly, soaking in Your blessed love. I giggle because You and I are together in Your wonderful presence, so Happy! The mention of Your Name is powerful, my words cannot describe. I am overwhelmed, so loved, powerfully filled, all because You are here. Is someone praying? I know I asked You to open heaven and pour many times, but today You answered. Was it our special time of worship, just You and me? Thank goodness for Walkmans.

Did You come home with me? It appears so, as on the verandah playing my simple love songs, Your Joy exploded inside me, and I have that smile that makes me feel like I have too many teeth in my mouth. I am so in love – with You. It's real heady and its heart and it's in my toes, must be because I keep wanting to dance – with You – for You. Hearing Song of Songs 2 read into my ears, like Your voice, speaking to me Words You had blessed me with repeatedly. I feel so high.

There is no gap in the clouds, I've checked but heaven is definitely open. My heart remains wide open to Your love my healer, who washes me clean. And to think – this is just a taste of You. How powerful You are. How sensational is Your love. Your presence is saturating me – I'm drowning in Your Joy… coming up for air. Are You having a wonderful time with me as I am with You? God, I love You. God, I love You. God, I love You. I am complete in You. You are all I need.

Katie flicked through the binder and found another that caught her attention and began reading it. She noticed her heart had changed she no longer felt teary or emotional, though it was taking her on a journey. It wasn't focused on the sorrow or loss, it was uplifting, it was all about the One she Loved and continued too.

I am accepted in the Beloved.

To the praise of His Grace wherein He hath made
us accepted in the Beloved. Eph 1:6

The greatest gift of all is –Love.
1 Cor 13:13
And this is our love story.
I am my Beloved's and His desire is towards me.
Song of Songs 7:10
Since before time- before His eyes were laid on mine
He knew me.
He orchestrated the music, the flowers in season.
The time, the place- knowing with His heart.
The Love we would
One day share

He has been wooing me from the beginning of all eternity.
But we were born worlds apart or so it seems to my heart.
And to His
I was made in dirt, – on this earth.
He in Love – in Heaven

So, You sent Your Son into this world.
Away from the Glory of You
And a voice came from heaven declaring.
"This is My Beloved Son in whom I am well pleased."
Matthew 3:17

And He was beautiful. He was just like You.
He only did what He saw You do.
And said what He heard You say.
He came out of Love - in obedience to You.
That I may know You – Love You
Find You
Romance You

Men and women of ages past
Left a journal and love letters.
They recorded Words of passion.
That You wanted me to have- to treasure always
And each new day You sing to me.
And I read Your thoughts.
You loved me so and always will.

It is then I realise the depth of Love You have for me.

As I read and my heart cries with what You all
went through.
Father Your Love was 'powerful' beyond my understanding as
You asked Your Beloved Son to lay down His life for me.
His Love was 'without measure' to say "Yes."
O gentle Holy Spirit
How great is Your Love and Your pain inside the Beloved?

I can hear what sounds like rain falling from the day Jesus died.
The sound echoes in my ears
It is the sound of Your Love being poured out.
And flowing to the dirt below
All over me it rains – thank You.

This beautiful Son - Jesus
Opened the door and showed me the way to Your heart.
Only through Him could I find my way to You.
I believe in Him though I have never seen Him 1 Peter 1:8
And I believe in You- I love You.
You allowed me to be accepted in Your Beloved
It was Your heart's desire- it was Your great pleasure.

My lips drip as the honeycomb Song of Songs 4:11
The last delicacy Jesus placed to His lips Luke 24:42
Before leaving to prepare a place for me John 14:3
To worship means to kiss
How else, I wonder could my lips taste of Yours
You whom I have never seen.

Yet as I read
the passages of time stretch out before me.
And I am lost in each page.
All are my memories, and I smile when I recall the
day I discovered – You were my poet.
When You spoke to me That those who revere Your Name the
Son of Righteousness would rise with healing in His wings
Malachi 4:2
I sweetly trace back in my mind and heart.
The day You revealed to me.
The face of Wisdom
Wonderful Proverbs 8
And I took it with me everywhere- laminated to protect the beauty that will never fade.

Still, I wait longing for more than a glimpse of You.
And You remind me by the power You left within me.
Of those times You were with me – so completely.
I laughed through the pain and danced with Joy.
Because You were with me
Silently You came into this world.
I alone knew that I had You?
That You had come for me
because I needed You

I was clothed in Your Presence
Washed in Your Love
I am filled with a hunger for You – I thirst for You.
You made a way for us.

For the tender moments in my now
And You draw me increasingly to the secret places.
where we meet
Because You ache for me
And yearn for me- as I for You
You've waited such a long time.
"Just a little while" I hear You whisper.

Katie put the binder down, she felt so much brighter like something had lifted off her. Then she recalled how He had used the very words she had written about Him and the Love she had declared to Him in the past and it had set her free then too. It was all there in her journals. And He had confided in her that was why He gave her a love to write. So, she would never forget no matter what the season, the journey she had shared with Him, and the love they had for each other. Katie smiled recalling that memory, He wanted her to capture it all.

CHAPTER 9

Lost And Alone

Nothing prepared Katie for the battle that was brewing, the sweetness was lost, and the questions and thoughts intensified. It was the saddest place, and she was consumed with it. It was like a switch had been turned on, like an accelerator on full throttle, like sinking down in the ocean with massive waves crashing over her and not knowing which way was up, she couldn't breathe. When she tried to share it, what her feelings and thoughts were, it magnified them, and no one seemed to understand and that included herself. And onward she ventured in The Fast and yearning for more of Him.

Instead of feeling peaceful she was edgy, and thoughts of loneliness washed over her continuously as she walked out of the church into the café, and her eyes were drawn to all the people standing with others, husbands, wives, children, grandchildren. Though she tried to reason it and remind herself she had been years on her own, not just a week or a little more, it didn't break the power of it. She woke sad, she walked sad and sang her love songs with emptiness and felt so alone. Even at work the thoughts penetrated her heart and she felt so alone and vulnerable. She fought so hard not to let tears escape but didn't always win the battle.

The sorrow was over whelming. She questioned, was it The Fast? Was it the anniversary of her loved one's departure? She really didn't believe so as she had allowed the Lord to deal with all of that. Was it fear, of health issues, dental expenses or work? It continued to such a place she could no longer think one positive thought about herself, and she started to partner with the thoughts, and it took her down even lower. Even her friends she always caught up with on Friday and Tuesday were busy that week and she was pleased as her heart was not in the right place. Every wrong word or action about herself was what she woke to, all her past was at the forefront of her mind to pull her down. It was loaded with guilt and regret. And though she talked to the Lord and repented the sadness remained.

Every situation was set up perfectly to create more havoc and disappointment and brokenness in relationships, and Katie cried and reached out for help, but it amazed her how many Christians did not answer their phones, they prefer text messages… In what she felt was a desperate need because the voice of the enemy was gently offering her a solution to her problems, she would take another walk along the river and pray in the Spirit as tears hidden behind her sunglasses fell. Is this the way the enemy attacks me, making me feel like a five-year-old girl insecure, under confident, lonely, vulnerable, always fragile in the heart and the emotions?

REMEMBER WHO YOU ARE

Katie sat on her prayer chair in the sunshine and read her Bible and talked to her Lord and thought perhaps there was another in the church going through similar. So, she asked Lovely Holy Spirit to help her, and she wrote prophetic messages of words of encouragement to her sisters and brothers in Christ. It just poured out of her and one by one she sent them off and knew this is a gift, an anointed gift He had placed upon her life and Katie absolutely treasured it.

She drank her coffee in the sunshine and watched as her cat wandered around the garden, it was peaceful and doing something she loved to do had helped a little, her mood had brightened. She prayed as she sent them and hoped they would touch the people she had sent them too. And so suddenly the blue light came on – on her phone telling her she had received a message.

"Oh, Katie this is exactly what I needed today, your timing is amazing."

Then as she continued to sit and drink her coffee the text messages came flooding back.

"Thank you, I was just asking the Lord a question, and this came through, wow thank you."

"That is so beautiful, thank you for sharing it."

"Katie, I have told you so many times you really have a gift to write, so prophetic, beautiful so beautiful. Love you honey xx Cassie."

Suddenly Katie thought of the dream and a chill went through her, the trembling Fear of the LORD. It all cascaded back on her, like a compelling desire to lay down prostrate on the grass before Him. His voice from the dream echoing in her heart, so authoritative and powerful, it was the question He was waiting on her to answer.

Silent tears ran down her cheeks. She thought again of the morning of waking in such joy like someone had shared a wonderful story with her all night long. Katie was aware so instinctively that she already knew what was revealed to her, but something was blocking her from recalling any of it.

MARY AT HIS FEET

Katie so looked forward to getting to church, it was all worship just loving and adoring Him. Three mornings and three evenings, she missed the night before as after her dentist appointment she felt so tired, it was only lunch time, so she laid down for a rest and woke at one thirty in the morning, so disappointed, and over and over she repeated that she was so sorry. Katie went to the morning worship, it was wonderful and all day all she wanted was to be back at the church He had called her too, and she knew without a doubt it was to worship Him.

It took place about two years ago when she was involved at a church but during the week, she would attend another church ladies meeting. On one morning she had such a prompt to walk to the church doors and as she did, His powerful presence brought her to tears. She pushed on the doors and took a breath, no one was in the church it quite dark, but Katie knew the church building well, she had a lot of memories at this place. It was like an unseen hand was leading her to the very front row and she sat and cried and cried, His Glorious Presence totally moved and enveloped her. She was reminded of all the years of worshipping Him right there, of all the places He touched her and delivered her and danced with her, through what was the most difficult season of her life.

It was at home alone she learned what it was to experience passionate intimate worship, she knew how to enter His presence and sing her own love song to her God that she loved, but corporate worship was something else. As she left the church that day, before heading into the ladies meeting, she asked Him, "Would You like me to come here on Sunday?" and like a bolt of electricity He confirmed. It was when she had come back after a few months He spoke to her again and said, "I never asked you to leave." He reminded her of a conversation she had had with a dear friend who had told her it was time to go, and so in obedience to what her friend had said she left.

Katie had wandered like a lost sheep from church to church looking for something, always loving to hear the Word being preached, and loving to worship, but as she reflected, she knew you cannot have peace or real contentment when you are out of alignment, she might have been in His acceptable will but definitely not His perfect will. How quick He is to forgive as we repent, it was immediate and she found what she had been wanting, pursuing passionately, it was to worship Him, to sing with all her heart, and to use her very body to express her love for Him.

Now all these years later, Katie found a place halfway down the church for the last night of the worship and prayer. She took an aisle seat as she always did so she could dance or kneel or whatever came to her heart. And as always, she sat alone, she looked around the room and was pleased with how many had come to worship. The presence of God was beautiful, and Katie loved every moment singing, dancing, bowing, and thanking her precious Lord. She dropped to her knees and sang to Him her own love song as the church sang theirs, she would sing with them all and then sing the words on her heart. The tenderness of worship was everything, Katie was in her favourite place, nothing could ever be as beautiful to her as worshiping Her King. She looked around for the briefest moment at all the people and suddenly it dawned on her, she was not lonely.

It was such a powerful revelation as she took in the truth, she was not lonely and it came so deep to her heart and mind that she never was, it had all been a lie. It was like a light going on and things breaking off her as she sang even louder and loved Him even more fully. For one week and three days she had believed the lie, and it wasn't until she was with Him in such intimacy pouring her love over Him that she got free.

"This is me, the real me, just adoring You, oh dear God how could I have believed such a toxic lie. You are everything I need, You, are always with me, I am never alone and never have been, I'm so sorry I believed the lie. God, I feel so free, I feel like me." Katie knelt lower into the carpet whispering her heart, knowing He was listening.

Suddenly her mind took her back and she could see herself walking out of the church that day as she noticed all the people with husbands, children, grandchildren and knew the enemy had planted not just the thought but the emotion behind it. She had been ensnared by what she saw and what she felt, and the enemy had known her so well to know how to attack her and bring her down on the very anniversary of her late husband's death. It was all a lie. Suddenly Katie saw it for what it was, witchcraft and a spirit of intimidation. Katie wasn't sad, nor was she lonely.

Katie smiled as she realized the gift the Lord had given her that night, it was Truth, He Himself had said *'the Truth will set you free,'* so she continued to sing love songs to Him, then someone was touching her arm. Katie opened her eyes to see a lady she had met once leaning down to her. "I have a word for you from the Lord, He said, 'you are like Mary at My feet, she pours love all over Me." Katie grabbed a hold of the lady's hands and spoke to her saying," This, is for the Christ in you," and she kissed her hands and held them to her cheeks knowing her Lord was receiving this gesture of love.

CHAPTER 10

To Kiss You

"God they never should have told me that to worship in Greek is to kiss, it's the only place for me, kissing You laying me down at Your feet. The only place of real freedom for me is in extravagant worship, the only place I truly belong and am satisfied. Face to face with You, You're all I see, my attention, my devotion, all that I am I simply give to You. It's the place I can breathe, it's in Your presence, Your river, Your Glory. It's You, You are what I want, all the rest is empty, I tasted and found You are good."

Katie drew part of the cross on a page in her notebook only one plank of wood from the dust of the earth to the heavens, its love, all for You. She drew lilies and a rose scattered across the page, and a single lily laid at the foot of the cross, instinctively Katie knew she was that, Lily. And a seed falling to the ground, "I will water it with my tears."

Katie stared down at the page and was stunned by what she saw in that brief second, it was a ladder from the dust of the earth to the heavens.

"You sent Your son into the world - for the world, and its powerful and truth, Your arms were reaching out on a beam of wood and Your hands nailed, and though I want the whole world to experience and know the wonder of Your love, I'm consumed in my love for You. Nothing compares and nothing else can fill me as You do. I just want to love You more; I want to give You more. I know now, the breaking, the emptiness, if I have nothing but You, I have it all.

Katie went and picked up her guitar and turned her phone on record, the chords were simple the words were her heart.

Your eyes upon me, my eyes upon You. Your eyes upon
me, my eyes upon You. You in me and I in You. You
in me and I in You, You in me and I in You.

God so loved the world that He gave me You. You were nailed
to the cross, You were nailed to the cross, and I was nailed with
You, I was looking, I was looking at You, nailed to the tree. Your
love, Your light, Your love, Your Light, Your Holy love.

I was looking at You; You were looking at me, I was breathing You in, You were breathing in time with me. I was breathing Your love, I was tasting Your love, You were dying for me.

You said, "I died to show the world, I die to show the
world, how much I love the Father, how much I love
the Father, I was dying – revealing My love."

My Heart, do this and remember Me, do this, and remember Me. Eat My flesh and drink My blood. Do this and

remember Me, do this, and remember Me. Do this and remember My death until I come for you… till I return to you.

Oh, I want Your love, oh I want Your Holy love, oh
I want Your love, God I love Your Love
God I love Your love.
You in Me and I in You, draw near to Me and I will draw
near to you, draw near to Me, I draw near to you.
If I be lifted up, I will draw you, I'm draw-
ing your heart, I've been drawing your heart.

I was drawing you near to me, and there You were upon
the cross, Lifted high in holy love for the Father, for the
Father, in obedience and love for the Father.
And I climbed the tree, to look into Your eyes, my
feet upon Your feet, my face to Your face.

I hear You breathing. You gave me beauty, beauty for ashes.
For the joy that was set before You, You endured the cross,
for the joy that was set before You, You endured the cross,
and the shame and the spitting and the mocking Lord.

God You were lifted high, I was lifted with You, crucified the hidden one in Christ. Face to face, Your tears washing down upon me. Your breath I was breathing in, your breath I was breathing in.

Your every breath was crying out, Your every breath was breathing love, Your every breath was showing me – I love you; I love you; I love you. Abide in Me I'll abide in you, abide in Me, I will abide in you!

It's you in Me and I in you, it's you in Me and
I in you, it's you in Me and I in you,
I can hear Your heartbeat, I was leaning in against You, like
a lover leaning against the heart. Holy, Holy love
I breathed Your last breath.
I breathed Your last breath.
You gave Your life eternal life, to the world Holy One
You gave Your Life unto the world – I breathe.
You said keep your eyes on Me.
Saviour, saviour calling, Yeshua the Lord saves.
Saviour, saviour calling, Yeshua the Lord saves.
Save now – save now.
Holy, Holy are You.

Yet they couldn't see, they couldn't see the Holy man
lifted high from the land. They couldn't see the Son
of man the Son of God, the lion, the lamb,
They couldn't see You, they couldn't see You.

They couldn't see the King of the Jews, they couldn't see the
Son of God, they couldn't see the Son of man, they couldn't
see the Saviour on the cross. They couldn't see You.

God, I see You,
weeping, bleeding, crying,
weeping, bleeding, dying.
The Saviour pouring out His whole life so I could live, the world waits,
the world waits. The Saviour's come, He was lifted high, do you believe?
Do you believe?

Didn't I tell you, didn't I share with you, that if you would just simply believe. Didn't I tell you, didn't I share with you, that if you will just believe. Didn't I tell you, didn't I share with you, the secrets of My heart, that if you would just believe, you would see, you would see, the Glory – the Glory of GOD. The Glory, the Glory GOD.

Didn't I tell you, I Am the Light of the world, did I not show you, I Am the Bread of Life, did I not say to you, I am the Salt of the earth, did I not share with you, I Am The Prophesy, can you not, see Me now, the promised Lamb. The Lord will provide, I Am – The Lord will provide, I Am, can you believe?

Blessed are your eyes that see Me, blessed are your ears that hear Me, blessed are your eyes that see Me, blessed are your ears that hear Me. Blessed is your heart that's open, blessed, blessed are you child of God. Blessed are you, daughter, daughter, if you just believe, if you'll only believe, you will see, the Glory, the Glory.

Who is this son of Glory, who is this King of Glory, who is this King of Glory, the Lord God Mighty in battle? Who is this King? He is the Lord God, He is The Lord God, high, lifted high.

Despising the shame that was set before Him, He came, He came, knowing what would come. He would give His life to the whole wide world, if we would just receive, we can have Him,

Eternal life, He said, eternal life, is it to know My Father, the Father, the One true and Living God. My Father, the

Father the one true and Living God, and to know, - to know
You- to know the Son in whom You sent. Oh, to know.

You in Me and I in you, you in Me and I in you, you in Me and I in you
Breathe Me in, breathe in Holy love, breathe Me in
I'm making you an oak of righteousness, cling to Me
the vine, that you might bear much fruit.

Walk with Me, follow Me,
This is the place I bow My head; this is the place I breathe My last. This is the place the Saviour dies, this is the place I'm crucified, this is the place we surrender all, that we can live, for love that we can love - for You.

Eternity, Eternity, Eternity, Eternity beckons me, the door is open,
Jesus said, I Am the way, I Am the truth, I Am the Life, Jesus said,
I am the gate, I am the door, the door is open, the door is open.
He said, Come up here.

And I breathe my last as You breathe your last breath. I took
You in so deep, so deep inside of me, and I became one with
Holy Love. I Am Your temple, I Am Your temple, You dwell in
me, You abide in me, You live in me, I'm alive. He caused me
to come alive, You fill me, You fill me, You fill me with life.

So, I come up higher, to see these things Love
has revealed to me, Love show me,

If You have seen Me, you have seen the Father, if you have seen Me,
you have seen the Father, you look at Me, You see Him, you stare

into My eyes, My face, you've seen Him staring into Holy Love, staring into Spirit, staring into life and love. Staring at the face of God.

If you look at Me – you have seen HIM.

Katie placed the guitar on the carpet beside her and knelt before Him, in silence waiting. Slowly she made her way to her feet and prepared the communion elements, a small piece of bread and a crystal glass of grape juice. She placed them on a tray with a candle and a lighter and returned to her place on the carpet.

Katie sat on the carpet looking intently at the gift of love and remembrance. Suddenly a smile rose up from deep within Katies heart, she picked up the tray and said to her precious Lord, "I have a surprise for You, don't look," she giggled. She placed the tray on the kitchen counter with enormous joy in her heart.

COME DINE WITH ME

Katie moved like on air, such a lightness to her step, she chose a deeply intimate worship song and began to remove the few things on her dining table. She wiped the table and headed to the linen cupboard for a beautiful antique embroidered tablecloth. Though it was ironed when she had last put it away, this was something special, so she ironed it again, taking such care. Katie loved the feeling she got as she threw the tablecloth across the table, positioning it perfectly.

Katie went again to the cupboard and picked up the linen napkins and re ironed them. Then she went to her drawer and picked out the crystal napkin rings, taking her time with folding and fanning the napkins out and racing out the door to her garden and she picked two sprigs of Baby's

Breath and gently threaded the napkins and the Baby Breath inside the crystal holders. Katie knew this flower was a symbol of Everlasting Love, perfect for what she had on her heart, for this special night.

Long ago Katie had been blessed with a new set of cutlery, she had put them away for a special occasion so this afternoon she went and pulled them out and washed them. The knives, forks, and spoons were so beautiful and shiny.

Next Katie went to a box at the very back of a cupboard and picked it up with such care carrying it to the counter and slowly opened the box she had not looked in for many years. The emotions it stirred up in her heart made her draw breath. She slowly picked out piece by piece and laid them on the counter, wonderfully excited she selected two of everything, and carefully hand washed them. Katie picked up a clean tea towel and dried the plates and bowls and with a heart full of love she placed the pieces on the table.

Katie then knew in her heart it was time to use that treasured three-tiered cake stand made of crystal and to set it in the very centre of the table. Her thoughts had already galloped off to the florist she would need to go to, and the very flowers she would decorate it with.

With such an excitement she reached for her car keys and purse and raced out the door. She selected white Roses and white Lilies; the fragrance was incredible in the car on the way home. Again, her thoughts felt soft and creative, and she thought of making place setting cards to go at each end of the table. Katie smiled so large as the words came to mind what she would write on the card.

She pictured in her mind the white cards she already had at home with the embossed flower boarders, and she recalled the fine gold pen she had bought long ago, hopefully it will still work, she thought to herself. On her return home Katie placed the flowers in water and went to look for the white place cards and pen. She turned on her phone and listened as she heard the song, she had sung to Him, pouring love all over Him.

She felt incredibly intoxicated so happy as she wrote on the place cards, in calligraphy *Lord* and *Lady* in fine gold. Katie had such joy placing the crystal glasses and the long-stemmed candle holders with Baby Breath wrapped around the base. Preparing this table was stirring up feelings inside of Katie, it felt like she was falling in love again only deeper.

God revealed His vast display of Love on a God sized scale. The Cross can be seen from every angle every generation. It reaches all the way back to Adam and all the way to eternity and filling the whole universe with who He is - love. And the Mary's anointed Him with oil revealing their great love for Him, but Katie whispered so she could surprise Him, 'I prepare a table for You.' As a woman on her own the most intimate and loving gesture she could gift to Him was her heart and her home and her table, it was all for Him and she wanted it to be beautiful for her King.

It felt like a real date, she was nervous she had showered and dressed, makeup and hair done. She did the finishing touches to the table and cut the flowers, the lilies and roses and placed them with such an eye to detail upon the three-tiered cake stand, with Baby's Breath fresh from her garden cascading from each tier, the very centre piece.

Suddenly a strong thought came to mind and Katie went to the drawer and picked up the gold pen, then took her place card off the table and wrote, the very name He called her *Catherine*, just underneath the word, *Lady*. Placing the card back at her position on the table. And then she lit the candles, it was so beautiful.

GIFTS

Katie stood back just looking at the table when suddenly and so unexpectedly there was a knock at the door. She opened the door to find one of the ladies from her church. Katie opened the door to invite her in, but she declined, saying her and her husband were on their way out, but the Lord had prompted them to purchase this gift and asked them to give this to her from The Lord. The woman handed over a jewellery box and said her goodbyes. Katie was stunned. Then the woman, turned and called out to her, "We were not to drop it off this afternoon or this evening or even tomorrow, He was very specific it had to be at this time, now." With that the woman walked out to the car with her husband awaiting her. Katie walked back in the house and closed the door. She opened the box and found precious sparkling earrings and a matching necklace. "Lord oh Lord, thank You I wanted to surprise You tonight, wow, these are beautiful, I have to put them on now, will You help me?" She headed to the bathroom mirror bubbling over with deep, deep joy at such an awesome surprise.

The woman's voice echoing in her heart, "We didn't know if you would like them," and He said, "Get these, for her." Katie walked into her lounge room and twirled and twirled so wonderfully happy. Her fingers kept finding the necklace and just kept tracing it with her fingertips as she beamed with such joy.

"Lord, I have a surprise for You, I prepared a table for You," Katie picked up her bible and took it to the table and opened it to John 6 and started to cry.

CHAPTER 11

Entree

Before Katie took her seat at the table, she looked up from the Bible to the place she had prepared for Him, she wondered in the briefest moment should she pull out His chair. In a gesture of faith and love she walked around the table and pulled out his chair for Him to sit and then walked back to her seat and sat opposite Him. She then placed the Bible on top of her entrée plate.

Katie's eyes fell on the scripture

> *I am the Living Bread that came down from heaven to give My Life to the world.*

Katie thought of that moment in the garden when the Lord had commanded Adam,

> *of every tree in the garden, you may freely eat, but of the tree of knowledge of good and evil, you shall not eat, for in that day you eat of it you will surely die.*

Eve took of its fruit and ate and gave some to her husband. They died spiritually that day, as they ate of the fruit of that tree.

> *I am the Bread of Life; he who comes to Me shall never hunger and He who believes in Me shall never thirst.*

> *Do not labour for the food which perishes, but for the food which endures to everlasting Life, which the Son of Man will give you, because God the Father has set His seal on Him.*

Katie was led gently by the Spirit to Isaiah 55, reading and weeping,

> *Ho! Everyone who thirsts, come to the waters; And you who have no money, come, buy, and eat. Yes, come, buy wine and milk without money and without price. Why do you spend money for what is not bread, and your wages for what does not satisfy?*

> *Listen carefully to Me, and eat what is good, let your soul delight itself in abundance. Incline your ear and come to Me. Hear and your soul shall live; and I will make an everlasting covenant with you - To give you all the unfailing mercies and love that I had for King David.*

Katie made her way back to John 6 her eyes fell upon the verse,

> *What shall we do, that we may work the works of God?... This is the work of God, that you Believe in Him, whom He sent.*

The big bold red letters were jumping off the page at her. This is the one who by faith was sitting opposite her at the table. A smile spread across her face as she thought of it.

> *As the Living Father sent Me and I live because of the Father, so he who feeds on Me will live because of Me. This is the Bread which came down from heaven, not as your father's ate the manna, and are dead. He who eats this Bread will live forever.*
>
> *Most assuredly, I say to you, unless you eat the flesh of the Son of Man and drink His Blood, you have no life in you. Whoever eats My flesh and drinks My Blood has eternal life, and I will raise him up at the last day.*

Katie read where the people responded saying,

Lord, give us this Bread always.

She felt the prompt of the Holy Spirit and followed His lead as she turned the pages quickly to Matthew 6 her eyes knowing exactly where to read.

> *Our Father who art in heaven Holy be Your Name, Your Kingdom come, Your will be done, on earth as it is in heaven. Give us this day our daily Bread.*

Like waves on the shoreline ebbing and flowing, backwards and forwards through His Word, Katie was continuously drawn back to John 6…

> *For My flesh is real food and My Blood is real drink. He who eats My flesh and drinks My Blood abides in Me and I in him.*

Through her tears Katie turned the pages knowing exactly where He was leading her, John 15.

> *If you abide in Me, and My words abide in you, you will ask what you desire, and it shall be done for you. By this My*

> *Father is glorified, that you bear much fruit, so you will be My disciples.*

Katie recalled the Power and Authority of His voice from the dream, this was not a scripture to be taken lightly nor for simple personal pleasures, this was so loaded with the backing of the Kingdom as the King had spoken. This was His purpose, His plans, His gifts, that we stir them up as Paul spoke to Timothy in both of his letters. That we use them in ministry – that we would truly bear much fruit.

Ask and you shall receive.

THE MAIN COURSE

Katie quickly got up from the table and broke off some bread and poured grape wine into her glass and sat back at the table, the presence of God sweet, but she knew there was so much more. It was like seeing the scriptures from all different perspectives and picking them up and seeing all the mysterious layers under each word.

Katie picked up the Bible and moved the entrée plate to the side and positioned the dinner plate in front of her and laid the Bible on top of it. Katie felt the strongest tug on her heart to head to John 11, she let her eyes skim over the familiar story of Lazarus, and the two sisters who sent word to Jesus, that he whom He loved was sick.

Once again Katie focused on the bold red letters as Jesus was speaking to his disciples,

> *This sickness is not unto death, but for the Glory of God, that the Son of God may be Glorified through it.*

The next words revealing how Jesus loved Martha, Mary, and Lazarus and yet He stayed two more days in the place where He was. After this,

He said, "*Let us go to Judea again.*"

Which concerned his disciples because the Jews had sought to stone Him.

> *"Are there not twelve hours in the day? If anyone walks in the day, he does not stumble, because he sees the light of this world, but if one walks in the night he stumbles, because the light is not in him. Our friend Lazarus sleeps, but I go that I may wake him up.*

Katie read how the disciples said to Him, *Lord if he sleeps, he will get well.* Bold, direct and to the point

> Jesus said, *Lazarus is dead. And I am glad for your sakes that I was not there, that you may believe, let us go to him.*

Katie scanned the lines to a place that always touched her,

> *As soon as Martha heard that Jesus was coming, she went out to meet Him, Mary stayed behind at the house. Martha said, Lord if You had of been here, my brother would not have died.*
>
> *But even now, I know that whatever You ask of God, God will give You.*

Katie glanced up from the Bible and just spoke to the place she had set for Him. "I love that she ran to meet You, there were crowds of people, mourners, but not one could comfort her heart like she knew You could. Martha had heard of the miracles You had performed, blind eyes opening, the lame walking, the sick healed, she did have faith. If You had of been there, (is what she understood) her brother would not have died, she even believed that in that moment You, whatever You asked of God, God would give it to You."

Katie looked back at the Bible at the place with the red letters and read it aloud.

> *Jesus said to Martha, Your brother will rise again. Martha says to Him, I know that he will rise again in the resurrection at the last day.*

Again, Katie looked to the place opposite her at the table and spoke to Him, "Even in Martha's deep grief I imagine her thinking, See Lord, I did Listen."

> *Jesus said to her, I am the resurrection and the Life. He who believes in Me, though he may die, he shall live. And whoever lives and believes in Me shall never die. Do you believe this? Yes Lord, I believe that You are the Christ, the Son of God, who is to come into the world.*

In that moment there was no, "Blessed are you, flesh and blood has not revealed this to you." There was no, "Woman great is your faith" it does not even record that You smiled at the enormity of the revelation she confessed to believing. How quick she was to answer, *Yes Lord, I believe.* This was the place where the shadow of death was hanging low over her.

Then she went away and secretly called her sister Mary, saying, *The Teacher has come and is calling for you.* As soon as she heard that, she arose quickly and came to Him.

> *Now Jesus had not yet come into the town but was in the place where Martha met Him. When Mary came where Jesus was,*

and saw Him, she fell at His feet, saying to Him, Lord, if You had of been here, my brother would not have died.

When Jesus saw her weeping and the Jews who came with her weeping, He groaned in the spirit and was troubled. And He said, "Where have you laid him?

They said to Him, "Lord come and see."

Jesus wept.

Katie stopped reading, suddenly the room seemed so quiet, there was a feeling an atmosphere she didn't know how to explain, she drew in breath, it just all became so still.

A long time seemed to pass as Katie sat with her eyes closed, just imagining Him weeping. Wondering what He was thinking. What were His tears really about? Silent thoughts ambushed her mind, "Was it the death of His friend Lazarus, maybe but He knew He would raise him, was it the unbelief He picked up in the thoughts of those around Him, maybe but many on His journey had not believed Him. Was it the tomb - that in no time at all He Himself would be laid down in one?

Katie opened her eyes and read what the Jews had said,

See how He loved him!
And some of them said,

"Could not this man, who opened the eyes of the blind, also have kept this man from dying?" Then Jesus, again groaning in Himself, came to the tomb. It was a cave, and a stone lay against it. Jesus said, "Take away the stone."

> *Martha said to Him, "Lord by this time there is a stench, for he has been dead four days?"*
>
> *"Did I not say to you that if you just believe you will see the Glory of God?"*

Katie felt so deep in her spirit those words were for her…

> *They took away the stone from the place where the dead man was lying. Jesus lifted His eyes and said, "Father, I thank you that You have heard Me. And I know that You aways hear Me, but because of the people who are standing by I said this, that they may believe that You sent Me."*
>
> *Now when He had said these things, He cried with a loud voice, "Lazarus, come forth!" And he who had died came out bound hand and foot with grave clothes, and his face was wrapped with a cloth.*

Jesus said to them, "Loose him and let him go."

Katie arose from the table and took her time choosing some music to go with her last course. She placed the Glory instrumental CD in the player and lifted her hands in praise and thanks for the beautiful evening she was loving being a part of.

"Lord this night is for You, and You are taking me deeper."

THE ICING ON THE CAKE

Katie once again took her seat at the table, removed the dinner plate, and stared down at the dessert bowl, "I know what I would like to eat at this moment." Katie said, with a smile on her face.

She opened to Psalm 27 and began to read,

> *"One thing I have desired of the LORD, that I will seek; That I may dwell in the house of The LORD all the days of my life. To behold the beauty of the LORD, and to inquire in His temple… I will offer sacrifices of joy in His tabernacle, I will sing, yes, I will sing praises to the LORD… When You said, Seek My face, my heart said to You, Your face I will seek."*

Katie sat quietly drawn by the desires she had for Him. Slowly she turned the pages and stopped at Psalm 63, it was like turning the pages of a photo album or journal all the memories that were intwined in these psalms were catching in her heart.

> *Oh God, You are my God; earnestly I will seek You. My soul thirsts for You, my body longs for you. In a dry and weary land where there is no water.*

She looked over at His place setting and just shared her heart as it overflowed, "Do You remember I used to sing this over and over to You? It brought me such comfort; my eyes and thoughts remained on You. You were my resting place and my anchor, and You came and bound up my broken heart."

> *I have seen You in the sanctuary and beheld Your power and Your Glory.*

> *Because Your Love is better than Life my lips will glorify You. I will praise You as long as I live, and in Your Name, I will lift my hands.*

> *My soul will be satisfied as with the richest of foods; with singing lips my mouth will praise You.*
>
> *On my bed I remember You; I think of You through the watches of the night. Because You are my help, I sing in the shadow of Your wings. My soul clings to You; Your right hands upholds me.*

Oh, beautiful Jesus, thank You, with all my heart, thank You, with all my love, thank You for all You have done, and those things You have planned to do.

Suddenly the wind picked up, and the curtains started to blow, it was like it was demanding her attention. Every open window was being flooded with such strong winds; the curtains even rose up as the wind carried them. And yet the candles did not blow out.

"Do You remember Lord, do You remember, after when everything changed, and I stood alone in the dark on the verandah of the home I once lived in. I was looking up to Your heavens and saw Your stars and gave You thanks and prayed, and a breeze picked up, I said to You how much I loved Your breezes. I closed my eyes and continued to pray, and the breezes got so strong it was like being out on a yacht in the ocean and I held onto the rails of the verandah, and I loved every moment, You, felt so close. Wow, I hadn't thought of that for a long time. The more I said how much I loved it, the greater the winds all around me." Katie said with tears running down her face.

"Oh Lord, it was the winds of change, I didn't recognise it then, it was just playful and fun, it was just those first days just learning how to breathe after… but it was more than that, wasn't it? You showed me my life was changing, never to be the same." Katie used her own hands to wipe the tears from her face.

"You are revealing that again, aren't You?"

And with that revelation, the winds died down.

Katie looked across at the bread and the glass of wine through her tears and yet with a smile. She turned the pages so quickly to Luke 24 and found the place she was looking for, where two disciples were walking along to a village called Emmaus and Jesus was walking and talking with them, but they did not recognise Him. He asked them questions and stated facts to them,

> *O foolish ones, and slow of heart to believe all that the prophets have spoken. Ought not the Christ to have suffered these things and to enter into His Glory? And beginning at Moses and all the prophets, He expounded to them in all the scriptures the things concerning Himself. When they drew near to the village where they were going, He indicated that He would have gone farther, but they constrained Him, saying, "Abide with us, for it is toward evening, and the day is far spent." He went in to stay with them. Now it came to pass, as He sat at the table with them, that He took bread, blessed, and broke it, and gave it to them. Then their eyes were opened, and they knew Him, and He vanished from their sight.*

Katie ate of the bread and drank of the wine, knowing in her heart though He had vanished from their sight, He was still there, very much with them… "Just as You are here with me."

Katie looked over to where He was sitting and smiled. Her elbow on the table, her chin on her hand and whispered, "Thank You, Lord."

CHAPTER 12

Out Of The Overflow Of The Heart

Katie woke happy and content, she didn't feel like a river walk so she fed the cat and sat out on her prayer chair in the sunshine, with a mug of white coffee. The cat followed her out and sat under the chair.

She thought about her wonderful evening with her Lord, so lovely, it surprised her that she could sleep at all with all the excitement in her spirit, but as she lay her head upon the pillow, it was like He bent down and tucked her in and kissed her on her forehead and immediately she slept, the sleep of the beloved.

Katie reflected on teachings she had heard lately believing and birthing a miracle, her heart was deeply stirred because every encounter with Him was more real nothing could compare, He was filling all the spaces in her heart.

Quite often lately Katie had heard friends pray and prophesy about the husbands they were believing for, the careers or the calls they would walk in, the home or businesses they would have. And as beautiful as that could be, something so delightful was moving her heart, suddenly she knew to go into the house and grab her phone and her guitar.

She tuned the guitar and turned the phone on to record knowing her heart would pour out what it needed too, there is such a freedom when music is playing.

Katie closed her eyes, and strummed, suddenly words flowed out of her open heart.

I'm not dreaming, I'm not conceiving, I'm not speaking, believing, or
even hoping for tomorrow's promises – not believing for a miracle.
I'm content here, full of love here. Finally found this
place, where I belong – with You – it's not yesterday. It's
not tomorrow, It's the simpleness of this place.

If it's too small for You – I'm sorry, but I have everything I
need – right here. I lack no good thing; my cup is full.

Because forever and always I run to You – I fell in love with Words.
The winds may blow upon these powerful Words, the rains
will water, and Your Son will always rise in my heart.

But there's no birthing – of a new day…
You're my Lily… You're My dream.
I have so much inside of me - this day. Thank You.
I'm not the anchor, I am the Lighthouse, and I will always shine for You.
And people passing by me will always see the
very image – the Light of You.

So, I live for love, I live for loving You. It's the sweetest secret
place. I'll light a candle; I'll come and sit with You.
I belong – I belong to You. I belong – I belong to You. Thank You.

Katie pushed stop on her phone and listened to the Words, the strong conviction of her heart. It was not going back to another man's hands or heart with all those memories, it wasn't reaching forward, for a miracle to make her complete. It was settled in her heart, she really wanted to choose to live with Him and know Him, like some of the great generals of the faith came to know Him.

She felt so empowered, all those years it was always ever present with her the thought of beginning again, like she had to. But she knew now she was not an add on to a dinner party or Christmas lunch, it's time she came out of the shadows and allowed herself to just be.

What happened was not the life she chose, and she had just tried to live through and find herself after the waves and through the years, and though she carried so much joy there was always the belief that she was not enough. Katie sat stunned at what rose up out of her heart, a silent tear was making its way to the corner of her eyes and then suddenly it hit her. "That's a lie." She flicked the tear away.

"It's a lie, Lord, isn't it? When did I start to believe that I wasn't enough?" Katie saw glimpses of her memories all the way through, even to childhood with each scenario reinforcing the lie she had believed. "Lord, oh my Lord, forgive me for believing such a cruel lie, would You help me and set me free of it, to live the truth from now on in courage, confidence, freedom, to really love who You created me to be. Lord there are so many lies that have caused me to be the person who lives only a quarter of a life, will You help me, can You truly transform me, like a makeover not for the outer me, but the very foundation of who I am. I'm in Your hands.

THE LILIES

Katie felt so blessed as she approached her church, those on the doors welcomed her with such warmth, as they did with everyone. She made her way to the second row from the front on the left-hand side, sat down and opened her Bible and her notebook and found her blue pen with expectation of a word or scripture, something she would need to record and remember. The worship team began to play preparing for the Prayer and worship before church began.

A lovely young family made their way to the front row and turned and signalled to her to come and sit with them. Katie quickly got up and hugged her friend and said hello to her husband and children.

'Oh Lord, Wow the very front row in Your presence, so, so happy.' Katie said under her breath with a big smile on her face. The children got up and raced outside to play, and Katie moved closer to the front and centre. She recalled all those years ago at a church held in a community hall when the worship was on and she left the room and danced in the adjoining room, twirling and singing with so much joy when a man came and took her hand without saying a word and led her to the front of the church, right at the centre. Katie sang a song that came on her spirit and knew in that moment that if the pastor had handed her the microphone, they would have heard her sing her heart of love to her Lord. Whenever she looked back on that day it was like that was her moment, to share her intimate worship.

Prayer and worship were powerful, wonderful and then the pastor preached, the presence of God so strong. He then invited anyone to come to the front to kneel or to worship and linger if they wanted to in the presence of the Lord. Katie felt compelled to step even further forward. All the congregation had the choice to go out for coffee in the café, to continue to worship but not to stay in the church and talk.

Katie was so captivated by His glorious presence and sung and moved with Him, this was everything worshiping Her Lord, with such freedom. She sang and danced and heard others around her, it was so beautiful, powerful the anointing standing beside those praising worshiping and singing, He was in the house.

When she finally opened her eyes, she noticed she was the only one remaining. It almost felt like Moses had left the tent of meeting and Joshua had lingered. Katie turned and stepped toward the place where she had sat and was so overcome with delight there on her seat was her Bible opened to Isaiah 60 and two white Lillies laid across the page. She read the header and smiled; The Glory of the Lord is upon you.

Though Katie knew who had left them, and that they came from Israel, she also knew deep in her heart they were from Him, it was like He had whispered to her, and she believed, "They are from Me."

Katie picked them up like the most precious of all gifts and headed out to the café, they were no longer making coffee, the congregation had left. She had deeply worshiped that long and yet it felt like minutes. Katie continued to love and worship Him as she wiped every chair and every table and cleared away the empty cups. Her attention and her eyes were constantly drawn back to the Lilies. And smiling her smile for Him.

YOU CARE

Katie's week was never busy it had just the right ingredients to keep it interesting, she felt so different about herself, and the way she was preparing the things coming up in the weeks ahead. It was the song that was birthed out of her and the realization that she was enough just on her own. She was not looking back, she was not looking forward, she was content, even more she was aware, she was never alone.

Even the very trip to the dentist was marked by His presence and though she opted not to have the Happy Gas she smiled and giggled as she left the dentist. He had been on her mind, and she drew strength from Him, He gave her so much peace.

It was at the pet shop the following day that she came to experience the wonder of His favour and provision. After just spending three hundred and forty-five dollars the day before at the dentist it was a shock to find out the flea and tick product would be one hundred and four dollars. Katie took a deep breath knowing He was with her and asked was there any chance of a discount as she had just spent so much the day before.

The cashier played around on her keyboard and said, "How about fifty-eight dollars?" Both the cashier and Katie were smiling so broadly the very presence of God so strong. Katie was so thankful to the lady but as she got in her car to drive away her heart of gratitude over flowed … for her Lord.

Katie went and did a small grocery shop ready for Christmas, cat biscuits and cat meat, fruit for herself and just the basics but she was so happy, back in the car she said to Him, "Lord we didn't get ham or meat or anything for Christmas lunch or dinner but I'm so content and thankful and You know how much I love fresh cucumber sandwiches. We are together and I'm happy."

One of her friends had already celebrated Christmas with their family so she would have been alone on the day, so Katie mentioned she would be welcome at her very simple lunch and that her river family had told her she was welcome to swim in their pool so bring her cozzies.

Every day God showed Katie His kindness and presence and her smile never left her face.

CHAPTER 13

Keys And Symbols

Katie began riding her push bike to work as the parking area was jam packed as it neared each day closer to Christmas, Katie loved the ride even though it had become very humid of late. She sang and prayed all the way; it only took about 30 minutes, and she arrived smiling and feeling full of Him.

One of the staff held the door for her as she put her bike out the back and then went to freshen up. It was then something caught her eye in the lunchroom with all the lockers. Right at the top was a white and blue Light House. Since her last trip to the Light House with her friends many months ago she was constantly seeing Light House ornaments, but this one was different, it had an adjoining room. This one reminded her of the scripture where Jesus had said "I go away and prepare a place for you," and following the culture of His day the bridegroom would go away and build a room on His father's house.

For some reason she had been compelled, so drawn to purchase these Light Houses as she saw them come in, all different sizes, some could even be lit up with a candle. Some of them had fishing nets attached to the sides with seagulls and one the largest one of all had an anchor. Katie loved the symbolism and knew there was a key, something she had to still search out.

It reminded her of something that was written down for her many, many years ago by a very dear friend. They were both on a discovery of God, to search for Him. 'I feel myself compelled to feel the power; the magnetism of the force too strong to pull from.' Strange to remember that all these years later at such a time, Katie thought.

He had revealed to her she was the Light House, but there was something about this compulsion to have these Light Houses before her eyes on display in her home. A friend had even seen a vision of a Light House as they spoke together over the phone. She had mentioned she saw the sun rising and setting on the Light House at the same time. She had asked Katie, "What do you get?"

"It is the beginning and the end, the first and the last." Katie spoke surprising even herself, but not really understanding.

As she started work that day, she went from one staff member to another to inquire who had put the Light House on top of the locker, how much it was, more importantly could she have it. No one knew anything about it, there was such a build of emotions racing through her and after a few hours she went out to the very back and asked the last person, it was a supervisor if he knew about it.

"Yes Katie, I put it aside for you the other day."

Katie was so excited and could not understand why and asked the price as well as thanked him.

"How's two dollars?" he replied grinning.

It made no sense, but it was overwhelming her, it was like just looking at the Light House was a message, but all she could do was smile and thank Him again and again.

PLACED UPON THE HEART

Katie raced to her bag to grab her purse and checked her phone, there was a missed call, so she quickly dialled the number.

She was stunned as a lady that did not go to her church had rung to say, "Katie the Lord had placed you on our hearts we have a gift box for you, with all the food you will need for Christmas day, for breakfast, lunch, and dinner. Will you accept it?"

"Oh, wow yes of course thank you, wow." Katie shared with her a little of the bills she had paid in that last week, but no one knew except her precious Lord what would have been on her Christmas table. The woman replied she would drop them off on the weekend and Katie got off the phone and cried.

Katie paid for the Light House with the adjoining room and went back to work trying to dry her eyes, and anyone who asked was told about the very goodness of God that can overwhelm and bring you to tears.

Those that said they had never experienced anything like that, she gushed "Well I pray you will experience the wonder of Him and His powerful goodness and love over this season."

It just flowed out of her. In the past she had prayed for boldness. but this was the overflow of a heart so completely undone with His love. Her whole day was so caught up in such a move of the Spirit, as she shared with everyone what the Lord had done for her and was so willing to do for them as well. It was so joyous even the ride home was like soaring on the winds.

A KING AT HER TABLE

Katie was woken by her cat at 5.30am Christmas morning and woke with such peace and joy. She opened the back door for the cat to wander out and then put on the kettle, put food in the cat's bowl, made her coffee and grabbed her Bible, she placed all the items on a tray and headed out the back door.

Katie spent hours happily praying and chatting and laughing and reading and just enjoying her Lord. She could not stop thanking Him for everything, her heart was so full of love, peace, and joy, it was the happiest Christmas she had experienced for years probably ever. It was all because of Him, the One her heart adored, the One her eyes had never seen but she did believe it was possible.

She had her toast on the swing seat in the sunshine with her cat and her Lord so content just enjoying Him. Happily, she read aloud the first five chapters of Luke and prayed for anyone who came on her heart.

When she came inside, she began to set the table for lunch and laid a red tablecloth and then a white lace tablecloth over that. She had so much fun putting all the finishing touches on and then had a silly idea to put a crown at the head of the table; it was one she had used on communion tables in the past.

When her friend arrived, she got a delightful surprise to see the table and the beautiful food that the Lord had provided, the excitement from Katie rubbed off on her friend and they had a wonderful time celebrating together.

After their lunch they walked down to the river and to the home of her river family for a swim in their pool. Katie could not stop continuously throughout the day thanking the Lord, it was such an incredible day, His presence so lovely and strong, she was always aware of Him.

It was simple and yet incredible they came back and had dessert and when her friend left, Katie returned to her place in the back yard with Her cat and Her Precious Lord, singing to Him and thanking Him.

Katie had a prompt to look at her phone and the message she read caused her to smile… 'How was your meal with your King?' The friend who wrote it never knew she had set a crown for Her King at her table.

'But He did.'

CHAPTER 14

A New Season

The season came to a gentle end, even the colour Dusky Pink reminding her of the book of Ruth and sweeter love and intimacy changed. Katie had been drawn to the Dusky Pink for a few months, everything that caught her eye like dresses, towels, and underwear, floor mats, blouses, T-shirts she felt drawn too, she tried to understand the significance of the colour and season.

Then suddenly Katie felt it in her morning walk along the river on the 20th of February, there was such a shift in the climate, noticeable and she knew the end of a season had come and the new one was on the very beginning edges. That day at work her heart and eyes were drawn to a new colour much softer; she picked out a pretty apricot - peach colour dress, that night she hand washed it and wore it the next day. No one had to tell her a new season had already begun. The heat and humidity of summer was over, at least for her.

There was also something else that was very telling, since that day all that time ago at The Light House, the day with the little girl, Katie had collected many Light Houses, and they had been on display all around her home. But suddenly she knew it was time to put them away. Like she was so close to unravelling what it was all about. She was well pleased but also had an unction that her life was going to change when she really understood the way He was speaking to her. As her friend had said a long time ago, "God has done all this to get your attention was there something He was getting you to look at?"

LOOKING IN THE MIRROR

Katie had been sick during the night, but she woke feeling excited, she did not at first have much energy but as the day progressed she sparked up.

It was a beautiful day, it was the first day of March and the wind was blowing and the sun shining, there was a magpie just near her front door singing and she loved the song, it reminded her of holidays as a child with her whole family.

Katie opened the Word and went to one of her most favourite books of the Bible, Genesis anything on Abraham delighted her heart so much, she could read and read it and never tire of it. Sometimes as she read, she would start at the end of Abrahams story, and she would hear Holy Spirit ask her a question and she would go backwards through the chapters as He answered through the Word. Blessed was she when she had a four-day weekend to be totally consumed with Him. Not leaving the house at all.

Katie was so content just looking at Abraham's life and how God spoke about him and to him.

> *The LORD had said, Shall I hide from Abraham what I am about to do, since Abraham will surely become a great and mighty nation, and in him all the nations of the earth will be blessed. For I have chosen him, so that he may command his*

children and his household after him to keep the way of the LORD by doing righteousness and justice, so that the LORD may bring upon Abraham what He has spoken about him.

Another time God spoke to Abraham,

Take now your son, your only son, whom you love, Isaac and go to the land of Moriah, and offer him there as a burnt offering on one of the mountains of which I will tell you.

So, Abraham rose early in the morning and saddled his donkey and took two of his young men with him and Isaac his son; and he split wood for the burnt offering and rose and went to the place of which God had told him.

On the third day Abraham raised his eyes and saw the place from a distance.

Abraham said to his young men, "Stay here with the donkey, and I and the lad will go over there, and we will worship and return to you."

Abraham took the wood of the burnt offering and laid it on Isaac his son, and he took in his hand the fire and the knife. So, the two of them walked on together.

Isaac spoke to Abraham his father and said, "My father!" and he said, "Here I am my son." And He said, "Behold, the fire and the wood, but where is the lamb for the burnt offering?"

Abraham said, "God will provide for Himself the lamb for the burnt offering, my son." So, the two of them walked on together.

Then they came to the place of which God had told him; and Abraham built the altar there and arranged the wood, bound his son Isaac, and laid him on the altar, on top of the wood.

Abraham stretched out his hand and took the knife to slay his son.

But the angel of the LORD called to him from heaven and said, "Abraham, Abraham!" and he said, "Here I am."

He said, "Do not stretch out your hand against the lad, and do nothing to him, for now I know that you fear God, since you have not withheld your son, your only son, from Me."

Abraham raised his eyes and looked, and behold, behind him a ram caught in the thicket by his horns; and Abraham went and took the ram and offered him up for a burnt offering in the place of his son.

Abraham called the name of that place The LORD Will Provide, as it is said to this day, "In the mount of the LORD it will be provided."

Then the angel of the LORD called to Abraham a second time from heaven, and said, "By Myself I have sworn, declares the LORD, because you have done this thing and not withheld your son, your only son indeed I will greatly bless you, and I will greatly multiply your seed as the stars of the heavens and as the sand which is on the seashore, and your seed shall possess the gate of their enemies.

> *"In your seed all the nations of the earth shall be blessed, because you have obeyed My Voice."*

Katie felt the prompting to head into the book of James and read,

> *Was not Abraham our father justified by works when he offered up Isaac his son on the altar?*

You see that faith was working with his works, and as a result of the works, faith was perfected and the scripture was fulfilled which says,

> *And Abraham believed God, and it was reckoned to him as righteousness," and he was called the friend of God...*

Abraham believed – He obeyed...

Katie was enjoying the incredible leading of the Holy Spirit as she turned to the book of Samuel and began reading where Samuel the prophet is saying to Saul the king,

> *"You have acted foolishly; you have not kept the commandment of the LORD your God, which He commanded you, for now the LORD would have established your kingdom over Israel forever.*
>
> *"But now your kingdom shall not endure. The LORD has sought out for Himself a man after His own heart, and the LORD has appointed him as ruler over His people, because you have not kept what the LORD commanded you.*
>
> *The word of the LORD came to Samuel, saying "I regret that I have made Saul king, for he has turned back from following Me and has not carried out My commands."*

> *Samuel said to Saul, "Why did you not obey the Voice of the LORD, but rushed upon the spoil and did what was evil in the sight of the LORD?"*
>
> *Samuel said to Saul, "Has the LORD as much delight in burnt offerings and sacrifices as in obeying the Voice of the LORD? Behold, to obey is better than sacrifice, and to heed than the fat of the rams. For rebellion is as the sin of divination, and insubordination is as iniquity and idolatry. Because you have rejected the Word of the LORD, He has also rejected you from being king."*
>
> *Saul said to Samuel, "I have sinned; I have indeed transgressed the command of the LORD and your words, because I feared the people and listened to their voice."*

Saul did not believe – he disobeyed.

> *After God removed Saul, He raised up David to be their king, concerning whom He also testified and said, "I have found David the son of Jesse, a man after my heart, who will do all My will."*

David believed – he obeyed.

The Holy Spirit took Katie on a deeper journey as she found herself reading from the book of Numbers and Exodus knowing it was about God's relationship with Moses.

He said,

> *"Hear now My Words; if there is a prophet among you, I the LORD, shall make Myself known to him in a vision. I shall speak with him in a dream.*

> *"Not so, with My servant Moses, He is faithful in all My household; with him I speak mouth to mouth, even openly, and not in dark sayings, and he beholds the form of the LORD. Why then were you not afraid to speak against My servant Moses?"*
>
> *Whenever Moses entered the tent, the pillar of cloud would descend and stand at the entrance of the tent; and the LORD, would speak with Moses.*
>
> *When all the people saw the pillar of cloud standing at the entrance of the tent, all the people would arise and worship, each at the entrance of his tent.*
>
> *Thus, the LORD used to speak to Moses face to face, just as a man speaks to his friend.*

A powerful surge went through Katie as she raced through the pages until she came to Philippians it felt like her heart was exploding on the inside as she was led to

> *Christ Jesus who although He existed in the form of God, did not regard equality with God a thing to be grasped, but emptied Himself, taking the form of a bond servant, and being made in the likeness of men.*
>
> *Being found in appearance as a man, He humbled Himself by becoming obedient to the point of death, even death on a cross.*
>
> *For this reason also, God highly exalted Him, and bestowed on Him the name, which is above every name, so that at the name of Jesus every knee will bow, of those who are in heaven and on the earth and under the earth, and that every tongue*

> *will confess that Jesus Christ is Lord, to the Glory of God the Father.*
>
> *This is the one who said, "The Son can do nothing of Himself unless it is something He sees the Father doing. I only speak what I hear the Father say."*

Jesus Himself said,
"Love is obedience."
The first Adam did not obey.
Before going to the cross, Jesus said to His disciples,

> *"You heard Me tell you, I am going away, and I am coming back to you. If you really loved Me, you would have been glad because I am going to the Father, for the Father Is greater and mightier than I am.*
>
> *And now I have told you before it occurs, so that when it does take place you may believe and have faith in Me.*
>
> *I will not talk with you much more, for the prince of this world is coming, and he has no claim on Me, he has nothing in common with Me.*
>
> *But I do as the Father has commanded Me, so that the world may know that I love the Father and that I do only as the Father has instructed Me to do.*

Jesus the last Adam - loved and obeyed always.

Katie closed the Bible and headed off to bed, she knew without a doubt why He had taken her on this journey.

Tomorrow, she must answer Him.

As Katie laid her head on the pillow a thought came, 'Will I see Him?' And just as quickly came the reply, "The just shall live by faith, and faith comes by hearing and hearing the Word of God."

COMMUNION AT THE LIGHT HOUSE

Katie woke early, His presence was so strong in her bedroom, it was like He was waiting on her to wake, and she thanked Him and very much welcomed Him.

She knelt beside her bed and quietly said, "Help Jesus." It felt in that moment she was breathing Him in, and it brought her such peace. "You lead me this day, I want to follow You, like You're one step ahead but Your hand in my hand is guiding me, Your Holy Spirit speaking into my heart." Katie stayed such a long time by her bed enjoying Him, and then in the stillness of her soul she heard, "Arise."

In her heart she had a picture of the Light House and knew this was where, He was asking her to go, and just as quickly without words He reminded her of a communion box that she had been blessed with almost 20 years ago, it had a miniature bottle for the juice and 6 tiny glass cups and a very small trinket box for the bread.

Katie had a nervous excitement as she located the communion box on top of the cupboard in the garage, it was with all the other treasured things she had used over the years for communion table displays. 'He never forgets a thing,' she thought to herself.

Katie quickly dressed as the kettle boiled, she raced back in and fed the cat, made the coffee, and poured juice into her miniature bottle and broke off a tiny piece of bread. She grabbed her Bible and her guitar and her guitar tuner and tossed all the items in her car.

"Holy Spirit it's time to return to The Light House with answers, I'm so glad You are with me. I don't know what to expect but I know He waits on me and has for just over a year. I was afraid of Him, of what He spoke that night in my dream, and the Power of His Presence and the authority of His Voice. I tried to cast it all aside throw it to the waters below, but He sent a little girl, an angel. He didn't want me to cast it- He wanted me to answer, I'm so sorry."

'Fear not for I am with you,' Katie heard in her spirit.

Katie arrived at the carpark, no other cars were there, she grabbed the picnic rug from the boot and the old beach bag that fit so much stuff and placed everything inside and then grabbed the guitar and made her way along the path to the Light House.

Right at the top, beside the Light House she set her things down, she could see the ocean and the blue skies and the beauty of her surroundings, she could smell the salt in the air and the smell of the earth. It was like everything was heightened in that moment as she sat down on the rug smiling with anticipation.

Katie opened her Bible, and the words leapt off the page at her,

> *For those whom He foreknew – of whom He was aware and loved beforehand – He also destined from the beginning… to be moulded into the image of His Son and share inwardly His likeness.*

Katie said again,

> *For those He foreknew,* that's what You said, You knew me and spoke over me before I was even conceived in my mother's womb. You spoke the very words- the plans You

> had for me, the purpose for my life and they were written in Your book in heaven.

"I heard You, the Words You spoke as if I had not been born yet, it was so powerful and enormous that You," Katie took a breath, "spoke it and imagined I could walk in it. I was dreaming but I knew it was real, I knew this is what had taken place, and You spoke to me, God You spoke to me." Katie started to cry releasing the fear and all her concerns, "You told me what You saw and what You wrote for my life in Your Son."

And then the gentlest Voice whispered through her, "Do You believe Me?"

Katie sobbed and reached for the communion elements and ate of Him and drank Him in, it strengthened her immediately. She stood up with the guitar in her hand not even concerned to tune it and sang, face to face with Him.

Like a whispered love song, Katie with tears streaming down her face, without all the fears and doubts of her limitations she once saw in herself, finally confessed what He had waited so long for, her words were so soft and yet she knew He heard her answer Him…

And His smile was felt deep within her, and her life would never be the same.

Because Love is Obedience.

Katie felt a prompt to reach into her pocket and to her surprise there was the stone, it caused her to smile as she pulled it out of her pocket, but no sooner was it between her fingertips it miraculously disappeared.

The End.

ABOUT THE AUTHOR

Carol Anderson loves the Lord and delights in reading, sharing, and walking closely with Him. Her greatest joy is living in His presence—through worship, prayer, and quiet moments spent with Him. Jesus is her all in all, faithfully sustaining her through sorrow, loss, and trials, and transforming them into beauty and blessing. Guided by the Holy Spirit as her teacher and friend, Carol's passion is deeper intimacy with God for herself and others. More than words on a page, He is her love story and the fullness of joy, inspiring her to write with intimacy and a sanctified imagination.

www.ingramcontent.com/pod-product-compliance
Lightning Source LLC
LaVergne TN
LVHW091008080826
845145LV00003B/1177

* 9 7 8 1 7 6 4 4 4 3 0 1 2 *